WEST METRO WINTER RECREATION

See inside back cover for EAST METRO WINTER RECREATION

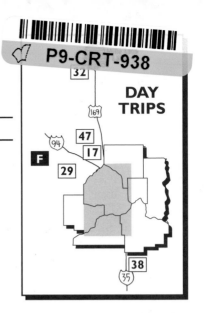

DAY TRIPS

7 **PARK** or **TRAIL** CROSS COUNTRY SKIING See pages 16 to 83

NOTE: 1 kilometer (km) = .62 miles (mi)

Z **DOWNHILL SKIING** See pages 84 to 97

SLEDDING (pages 114 to 119) , SKATING (pages 102 to 107)

SNOWSHOEING (pages 120 to 123) , WINTER CAMPING

BIRD WATCHING (pages 12 to 15), ICE CLIMBING (pages 98 and 99)

WALKING PATHS (pages 124 to 126) and SKI JUMPING (pages 108 to 113)

PARKS and TRAILS (See map on left)

2 ANOKA COUNTY TRAILS (pg. 28) 40 km ski   8.5 mi walk

  Bunker Hills Regional Park
  Chomonix Ski Trails
  Coon Rapids Dam Regional Park
  Lake George Regional Park

4 BAKER PARK RESERVE (pg. 31) 11.5 km ski

7 BLOOMINGTON TRAILS (pg. 34)   26.4 km ski

  MINNESOTA RIVER TRAIL   7 mi walk
  Girard Lake Park
  Mt. Normandale Lake Park
  Nine Mile Creek
  Tierney's Woods

8 BURNSVILLE SKI TRAILS (pg. 35)   15.7 km ski, 1 mi walk

  Alimagnet Park
  Terrace Oaks Park

10 CARVER COUNTY SKI TRAILS (pg. 37)   16.5 km ski

  Baylor Regional Park
  Lake Minnewashta Regional Park

11 CARVER PARK RESERVE (38) 21 km ski   6 mi walk

12 CLEARY LAKE REGIONAL PARK (pg. 39)   13.3 km ski

15 CROW-HASSAN PARK RESERVE (pg. 42)   17.6 km ski

18 ELM CREEK PARK (pg. 45)   14.7 km ski   4 mi walk
  NORTH HENNEPIN REGIONAL PARK

19 FORT SNELLING PARK (pg. 46) 16.6 km ski   10.8 mi walk

20 FRENCH REGIONAL PARK (pg. 47)   9.6 km ski

25 HYLAND LAKE PARK RESERVE (pg. 52)   9.8 km ski

    2 mi walk

30 LOUISVILLE SWAMP (pg. 57)   19 km ski

  Wilkie Unit – Blue Lake Trail

33 MINNEAPOLIS TRAILS (pg. 61)   11 km ski

  Columbia, Gross and Hiawatha Golf Courses   26 mi walk

34 MINNESOTA LANDSCAPE ARBORETUM (pg. 62)

35 MINNESOTA ZOO (pg. 63)   10 km ski, 1.5 mi walk

36 MINNETONKA TRAILS (pgs. 64,65) 16.5 km ski

    32 mi walk

  LRT TRAILS
  Big Willow Park
  Hopkins High School
  Lone Lake Park
  Meadow Park
  Purgatory Creek Park
  Victoria-Evergreen Park   STARING LAKE PARK

37 MURPHY-HANREHAN PARK RESERVE (pg. 66)

    19.4 km ski, 3.7 mi walk

44 RICHFIELD TRAILS (pg. 73)   10.5 km ski   3 mi walk

  Rich Acres Golf Course
  Wood Lake Nature Center

45 RITTER FARM PARK (pg. 74)   12 km ski

53 WIRTH PARK (pg. 82)   18 km ski

DAY TRIPS (See map above)

17 ELK RIVER SKI TRAIL (pg. 44)   15 km ski

29 LAKE MARIA STATE PARK (pg. 56)

    22 km ski, 3 mi walk

32 MILLE LACS KATHIO STATE PARK (pg. 60)   32.1 km ski

38 NERSTRAND BIG WOODS STATE PARK (pg. 67)

    12.8 km ski   5 mi walk

47 SHERBURNE NATIONAL WILDLIFE REFUGE (pg. 76)

  Sand Dunes State Forest   20 km ski 7.5 mi walk

DOWNHILL SKI AREAS

B BUCK HILL (pg. 89)

D HYLAND HILLS (pg. 91)

F POWDER RIDGE (pg. 93)

J WIRTH PARK (pg. 97)

The atmosphere in Minnesota in winter is like a wine,
so exhilarating is its effects on the system.

Minnesota, Its Character and Climate, 1871

Fred's Best Guide to

TWIN CITIES WINTER Recreation

Happy Trails!

Richard Fred Arey

By
Richard 'Fred' Arey

MINNESOTA

OUTDOORS
PRESS

Fred's Best Guide to
TWIN CITIES WINTER RECREATION

Minnesota Outdoors Press
Richard Fred Arey • 534 Laurel Avenue #6

612-290-0309
Saint Paul, Minnesota 55102

Additional copies of this book or *Twin Cities Bicycling* may be obtained by sending $18.50 per copy (price includes tax, shipping and handling) to the publisher at the address above. Make checks payable to Minnesota Outdoors Press.

I GET BY WITH A LITTLE HELP FROM MY FRIENDS.

Cover art and design – David Mataya

Production and design – Rob Schanilec – my main man

Word processing – Rob Schanilec

Text, maps and some illustrations – Fred

Editing – Julie Lund and Patty Frazier

Photos – Credits adjacent to photograph where known

First printing, 1996

10   9   8   7   6   5   4   3   2   1

Library of Congress Cataloging-in-Publication Data

Arey, Richard
    Twin Cities Winter Recreation
    Fred's Best Guide to Twin Cities Winter Recreation
    Richard Fred Arey
    p.   cm.
ISBN 0-9620918 - 2 - 0 $14.95

1. Winter Recreation – Twin Cities Metropolitan Area – Guide
    book
2. Minnesota – Twin Cities – Bird Watching, Cross Country and
    Downhill Skiing, Ice Fishing, Ice Climbing, Ice Skating, Ski
    Jumping, Sledding, Snowshoeing – Minnesota
3. History – Winter Sports – Minnesota

Watch for these upcoming Minnesota Outdoors Press books.
1. A Pictorial History of Twin Cities Parks and Recreation
2. Twin Cities Summer Recreation
3. Twin Cities Waterfalls
4. Saint Paul Winter Carnival — A Pictorial History

Inuit meditation is from *Eskimo Realities* by Edmund Carpenter ©1973. Reprinted by permission of Henry Holt & Co., Inc.

LIABILITY DISCLAIMER

Places and activities described and mapped in this book were compiled from a variety of sources. Minnesota Outdoors Press and Richard Arey assume no liability. The maps and descriptions are intended to aid in the selection of routes and activities, but do not guarantee safety while pursuing or engaging in them.

HAVE FUN, STAY WARM, RECREATE AT YOUR OWN RISK

DEDICATION

This book is for all who embrace Winter.

And I think over again
My small adventures
When with a shore wind I drifted out
in my kayak
And thought I was in danger.
My fears,
Those small ones
That I thought so big,
For all the vital things
I had to get and to reach.

And yet, there is only
One great thing,
The only thing:
To live to see in huts and on journeys
The great day that dawns,
And the light that fills the world.

Inuit meditation

WELCOME TO WINTER!

CONTENTS

This book is designed to help you discover the world of winter recreation waiting outside your doorstep. The Twin Cities offer a variety and quality of outdoor adventures as rich as any place on the planet.

These pages describe the simple pleasures of WINTER WALKING (page 124) and the high-tech excitement of ICE CLIMBING (page 98), the long tradition of ICE SKATING (page 102) to the latest innovations transforming the sport of SNOWSHOEING (page 120).

Over 800 kilometers (500 miles!) of excellent CROSS COUNTRY SKIING (page 16) trails are described and mapped in this book. St. Paul was the birthplace of SKI JUMPING (page 108) in this country, and both the Minneapolis and St. Paul Ski Clubs have excellent facilities for training young jumpers and competitors.

Ten DOWNHILL SKIING areas (page 84) make the most of every vertical foot to be found and many include state-of-the-art SNOWBOARDING (page 84) parks for kids.

WINTER BIRD WATCHING (page 12) is surprisingly good for bald eagles, trumpeter swans, turkeys, owls and a host of passerines that flock to bird feeders at nature centers everywhere. And no winter recreation book would be complete without a list of SLEDDING AND SNOW TUBING hills (page 114) that will bring a smile to the heart of every kid from 6 to 60.

I love winter. But, love it or leave it, if you live in Minnesota, one thing is for sure — when winter comes, it makes itself at home.

Winter starts knocking on the door around Halloween. In 1991, it busted down the doors when the famous Halloween blizzard dropped 28.3 inches of snow – our greatest single snow storm. December, January and February are the heart of winter, and March is our biggest snow month. The continuous snow cover season lasts from November 19th through March 19th, and in the Twin Cities we average over four feet of snowfall in a given year. As you can see, it will take more than a couple of hot dishes to see you through.

So relax. Take a deep breath. Remember back to when you were a kid and you'd go running out the back door to go skating, sledding or building snow forts with your buddies. Cold wasn't even a consideration and your mom would have to call out to make sure you remembered your mittens.

Winter defines us as a people and as a state. The hills, lakes, rivers and valleys we live amidst are mostly glacial formations. Long winter nights and snowball fights, 'CCO snow days and breath's frosty haze, pushing out strangers' cars, and skiing under the stars all drift markedly into the psyche. The first snowfall each year is magic. The trick is to embrace winter so that *every* snowfall is magic.

Courtesy of Dyke Williams

DRESS FOR SUCCESS

*T*here is no such thing as bad weather, only bad clothing.

Jim Gilbert, author of
Through Minnesota's Seasons

Learning how to stay warm and dry outdoors makes all the difference. Read this carefully, consult with a quality outdoor store and purchase footwear and clothing that will perform when you need it. Don't be cheap. Well-made gear not only does what it's designed to do, it lasts. My expedition mittens were purchased over 20 years ago and they still work great today.

You no longer need to look like the Michelin (wo)man when you recreate outdoors. Modern sports gear is sleek and colorful. Still, fashion is not the point, comfort is. If you prefer big mittens and bomber hats, go right ahead. They'll probably be the rage next season anyway.

The following pointers were written with aerobic sports in mind where moisture (perspiration) control is essential. For less aerobic activities like bird watching, sledding and walking you may prefer heavier wool pants or insulated overcoats with hoods.

Keeping your feet warm is always important. For years, Sorel boots, manufactured in Canada (they come in a variety of styles and ratings), have been the last word in warm winter footwear. As Garrison Keillor has written, "In my Sorels, I will be grateful for winter."

For the past decade Steger Mukluks in Ely, Minnesota (1-800-685-5857), have provided expedition-proven alternatives to Sorels. Using traditional designs and sturdy soles, they weigh half as much as traditional "pac boots." Here are a few sayings to remember:

Cotton kills! Managing perspiration in winter is essential. Polypropylene, Capilene, Olefin or silk do a great job of wicking away sweat so your skin is dry. Cotton doesn't. Wet cotton against the skin rapidly conducts heat away from your body. It can lead to hypothermia, which is the leading cause of outdoor deaths.

Don't be fat, wear a hat! This used to read, put on a hat (or two – see below) if your feet are cold. Estimates vary, but 30 to 80% of your heat loss can be through your head.

It don't mean a thing if it ain't got that swing! Walking, skiing, ice climbing – you need to move in comfort. Most sports clothing makers realize this, but check it out when you're in the store. Do your best Groucho walk or imitate the motion you'll be making. Does it feel good? Is it quiet? Can you move easily?

"DRESS IN LAYERS!"

The Minnesota Mantra – perhaps you've heard it before. It works, and though many people have heard it, few realize it is just as important for your head, hands and legs as it is for your torso.

When ski touring, you mix periods of activity (generating heat) with inactivity (eating lunch, checking out the view, etc.). You'll likely need to quickly put on or take off a layer as you go. A fanny pack or day pack is almost a necessity. It works best to add (or remove) a layer *before* you get too hot or too cold. Here are the three Ws:

Wicking Layer *The most critical, mix and match but no cotton or cotton blends.*

Warming Layer *Wool, poly pile and polyester fleeces all work fine.*

Protective Layer *Shells of Gore-Tex, coated nylon and even wool can be used.*

WICKING LAYER

Don't sweat it, this layer next to the skin will keep you dry by wicking perspiration away. It is the most important layer and should be worn toes to nose when it's cold enough.

WICKING MATERIALS: Thermax, Capilene, polypropylene, Olefin and silk all work great. Cotton and cotton blends shall not be used.

WARMING LAYER

Dry warm air is the secret to this insulating layer. The fur (hair) on caribou and polar bears is hollow, and when manufacturers were able to imitate nature's insulation they were able to create a variety of piles, blends and synthetics that will keep you warm.

And don't forget about the old standbys for this insulating layer. Wool still works great and can be less bulky than piles. Wool does hold more moisture though – 30 to 40% vs. 1% for polar fleece. If you perspire heavily, this is a consideration.

Many folks like a zippered turtleneck that allows some ventilation options. Be careful not to overdress your upper body at the expense of your extremities. Two thin warming layers often work best.

WARMING MATERIALS: Piles, Polartec and other polyester fleeces, wool, Thinsulate, Quallofil, PolarGuard, Hollofil II.

WIND AND WATER PROTECTIVE LAYER

The outer layer — and sometimes this is integral to the warming layer — must be windproof. For most winter outings in Minnesota rain is not a big concern and almost every shell will be able to shed wet snow. Breathable fabrics are preferred. Tightly-knit wools can be very wind resistant. Lightweight parkas with a hood can be kept stuffed in a fanny pack until they are needed.

Take no prisoners! Ready for winter's best shot, Maria sports a bomber hat, balaclava, goggles, expedition mittens and mukluks.

WINDPROOF MATERIALS: Gore-Tex, Triple Point Ceramic, Pneumatic (Activent) Windstopper, Stormshed, Klimate, coated nylon.

HEAD AND NECK

I am always amazed at the number of people walking around on the coldest days without a hat. You almost wonder where their head is.

Thirty to eighty percent of all heat loss is through the head, and experienced outdoorspeople understand that the layer concept is just as important for the head and neck as anywhere else.

I highly recommend having a silkweight, wool or synthetic **balaclava** (a pull-over, neck-covering face mask) stashed away **with you on all trips.** This will provide complete protection for the face and neck and can be rolled up for use as a simple stocking cap.

For most outings a **poly headband/earband** is all you'll need and it will hardly mess up your hair at all. When windchills drop below zero, you'll be glad you brought an ever-stylish **"bomber hat."** Gore-Tex and pile have replaced leather and rabbit's fur. The earflaps often wrap under the chin to provide maximum protection against exposure.

Most headgear will leave some skin exposed. Lotion **skin protectors**, such as Dermatone or Warm Skin, can be used on the face — even on the eyelids — where it is still exposed.

Goggles and complete face masks are available for downhill skiing or extreme conditions.

HANDS AND WRISTS

Keeping your wrists protected and warm is the first step toward warm hands. Layering — having a couple of options for your hands — makes a lot of sense. Thin **poly gloves** are fine when it's near freezing. Keep a pair of **thinsulate gloves** or **wool mittens** stashed away in case a cold front moves in or you start sweating. Gore-Tex overmitts complete the three W layering system. Many years ago I bought a pair of **expedition mittens** from Eddie Bauer that have kept my hands warm in the most extreme conditions. Like Sorels or mukluks they are a Minnesota must.

FEETS, DON'T FAIL ME NOW.

Feet seem to be the hardest extremity to keep warm. **Poly inner socks, heavy wool (ultimax-synthetic blends) outer socks** and boots that comfortably accept this extra thickness are essential. Boots that are too tight and restrict the circulation may be the biggest contributor to cold or frostbitten feet. **Mukluks** are warmest because they wrap your feet with no constrictions.

Washing your feet before you go out (you could shower!) will eliminate natural body oils so your skin will be as dry as possible to start. Replacing wet socks with dry ones during a long tour will also help.

Drink before you're thirsty and eat before you're hungry. Snack along the trail, or stop and enjoy lunch.

EAT HEARTILY

Will Steger, who's visited both the North and South Pole by foot and knows a bit about outdoor adventure, has two pieces of advice for folks heading out in winter: Dress properly and eat right. You'll burn more calories than you think and need a solid base to work from.

The best type of meal is one that is loaded with carbohydrates and fat rather than protein. A big bowl of oatmeal and butter does better than steak and eggs. Drink lots of juice or water as well.

If you are heading out for more than a couple hours you'll need to bring plenty of water (a quart per person in plastic containers wrapped in an extra sweater) and snacks – gorp, nuts, raisins, granola, M&Ms, baby carrots, etc. See the CROSS COUNTRY SKIING chapter, "Don't Leave Home Without It" section for a complete list of day trip niceties and necessities that can be carried in a fanny pack.

A winter picnic can be great fun if it's not too cold. Bring a plastic tablecloth (space blanket), paper towels, plastic bowls and utensils. Wide-mouthed insulated Thermoses and Tupperware containers may prove useful.

FOOD FOR THOUGHT

• Thermos filled with hot chili, cajun pork stew or hearty soup
• Deli sandwiches or ham and cheese croissants
• Brownies, homemade cookies
• Gourmet cheeses or smoked fish
• Good breads, bagels or muffins
• Baby carrots, dried or fresh fruits (orange sections become frozen popsicles — kids love them)
• Hard candy or candy bars
• Your favorite gorp mix (I combine a 12-ounce-tin of mixed nuts – no peanuts – with 12 ounces of beer nuts and about 8 ounces of raisins for a quick fix)
• At least a pint (preferably a quart) of water per person

RECOGNIZING FROSTBITE — Hypothermia page 22.

Frostbite occurs when the skin tissue completely freezes. It can happen in just a few minutes. It most often occurs in areas of least circulation and greatest exposure – nose, ears, cheeks, chin, feet, neck and hands. Frozen skin cells appear whitish, grayish or yellowish. Frostbitten skin will feel hard and very cold to the touch.

Prevent frostbite by being aware of the cold and looking for telltale white spots on the nose, chin, neck and cheeks of people you're with.

FROSTBITE TREATMENT — Seek medical attention!

• Do not rub with snow or anything else
• Dry, gradual warmth is preferred over immersion in warm water
• Warm frost-nipped skin by placing wrist against facial area, hands in armpits or groin, and bare feet on bare stomach (indoors)

WINTER DRIVING TIPS

The first winter driving tip is to use a front-wheel drive (or four-wheel drive) vehicle that is serviced regularly and has a good battery. Drive slower, brake sooner and keep all windows clear of ice and frost. Fill up the gas tank at the halfway mark and use a lighter-weight (5W-30) oil. Keep an extra gallon of windshield wiper fluid in the car and have arctic wipers installed as necessary.

The second winter driving tip is to dress as if you have to walk out. Since you're already, "dressed for success," this shouldn't be a concern. Still, many folks keep an old down jacket, Sorel boots, and a wool cap and mittens stashed away in the event they get stranded when they're not dressed for the outdoors.

The third winter driving tip is that if you do get stuck in the midst of a blizzard or winter storm, do not walk away from your car unless you can see other shelter. It is much easier to stay warm and get rescued if you stay where you are. You will, of course, have a sleeping bag, candle and matches, and some snacks to munch on while you wait. Make sure the exhaust pipe is not clogged with snow if you keep the car running. Leaving a window slightly cracked is a good idea.

Get out the mobile phone. Depending on the situation, call AAA, a tow truck, 911 or whoever is waiting for you at home. Relax. Order a pizza.

WINTER SURVIVAL CAR KIT

• Extra boots, wool socks, heavy coat, wool cap and mittens
• Windshield scraper and brush
• Jumper cables
• Snow shovel (hub caps work in a pinch)
• Sand/salt mixture for weight/traction
• Reflective emergency triangle or flares
• Blankets or sleeping bags
• Three pound coffee can with plastic lid that contains matches, candle, flashlight, granola bars (nuts, etc.), paper towels, aspirin, swiss army knife, large plastic bag, quarters, safety pins, first aid kit, whistle, pencil and paper, red bandana to hang on car antenna.

WINTER WEATHER

> *E*ven when it started to snow she did not lose her sense of direction. Her feet grew numb, but she did not worry about the distance. The heavy winds couldn't blow her off course. She continued. Even when her heart clenched and her skin turned crackling cold it didn't matter, because the pure and naked part of her went on.
>
> The snow fell deeper that Easter than it had in 40 years, but June walked over it like water and came home.
>
> **Louise Erdrich**
> Love Medicine

The 45th parallel of north latitude runs right through the Twin Cities. This means we're exactly halfway between the North Pole and the equator. But unlike the rain forests of Oregon or the wine country of France that share the same latitude, Minnesota is located far from the tempering effects of an ocean. While most people forget the often sweltering heat of summer (the Twin Cities' all-time high temperature of 108°F is hotter than Washington, D.C. has ever been), the length and strength of winter is never far from thought.

Tremendous blasts of winter affirm our place in the grand scheme of things. Even the word "blizzard" was first used to describe a storm that hit Minnesota and Iowa in 1870. From March 14 to March 16, a fierce storm dropped 16 inches of snow. An Iowa newspaper borrowed the boxing term for a volley of punches to describe the snow storm. And the 1-2-3 jabs of blowing snow, cold and greatly reduced visibility have been called blizzards ever since.

Twin Cities weather records themselves have a remarkable history. Dr. James Tilton, Surgeon General of the U.S. Army, decided back in 1814 to have remote army bases keep track of the weather. Deep in the wilderness, at the confluence of the Mississippi and Minnesota Rivers, the army post's medical officer began reading his thermometer in October 1819. The fort had just been established and it would be six years before it took the name of its second commander, Colonel Josiah Snelling. The Fort Snelling weather log, with subsequent Twin Cities record keeping, comprises the longest chronicle of precipitation and temperature in the interior of North America.

Setting global warming and your childhood memories aside for the moment, Minnesota continues to get its fair share of record-setting winter weather. Ground Hog's Day *always* means six more weeks of winter in this state, but on February 2, 1996, a 2-inch-high headline in the *Star Tribune* declared -60°F the coldest temperature recorded in Minnesota. The town of Tower grabbed the record, amidst no small controversy, and the townspeople cheered.

| Twin Cities Weather Forecast | 375-0830 |
| National Weather Service (local) | 361-6680 |

Here are some of the highs (snowfall) and lows (temperature) that have been recorded in the Twin Cities metro area. The information is from *Minnesota Weather* by Richard Keen, *Prairie Skies* by Paul Douglas, the Freshwater Foundation's annual *Minnesota Weatherguide* calendar, Bruce Watson, meteorologist, and Mike Lynch, WCCO Radio 830.

All-time low Twin Cities' temperatures
-46°F at Fort Snelling on January 21, 1888 (St. Paul hit -41°F for its record low the same day)

Consecutive hours below zero
186 hours – 5 p.m., December 31, 1911 to 1 p.m., January 8, 1912

Consecutive days below freezing (-32°F)
79 days – December 19, 1874 through March 8, 1875

Coldest windchill rating -77°F in 1977 (unofficial)

Earliest and latest reported snow flurries
The "possible snow" season is from Sept. 15 to May 28 – 256 days.

Average season with at least 1" snow cover
The "continuous snow cover" season lasts from November 19 through March 19 – 121 days.

Greatest snowfall
The 1991 Halloween storm set several records including greatest snowfall in a 24-hour period (20.4"), greatest snowfall from a single storm (28.3") and earliest snowfall over 8".

Snowiest winter in history
The winter of 1983–84 received a record of 98.4" of snow, including a 9.7" snowstorm on April 29–30 that was the biggest ever so late in the season.

Earliest and latest ice-out on Lake Minnetonka
March 11, 1878 and May 5, 1858. The average date is April 15.

There you have it, but just remember – records were made to be broken. Bruce Watson, Minnesota's best meteorologist, reports the following averages at his Roseville weather station over the "standard normalizing period" from 1961 to 1990.

	High	Low	Snow
November	39.7°F	25.0°F	7.8"
December	25.1°F	10.1°F	11.7"
January	20.6°F	3.5°F	11.9"
February	27.0°F	9.2°F	8.8"
March	39.1°F	21.6°F	12.2"
April	55.8°F	35.0°F	4.4"

In June 1996, the National Weather Service began using the Automated Surface Observing System (ASOS) for recording the weather. Experts believe this new system is less accurate and will record lower precipitation and temperatures than before. For example, in 1996, the ASOS recorded -34°F – tying the record – when the official (human) reported temperature was -32°F.

Hundreds of bald eagles spend the winter along the Mississippi River from St. Paul south to Wabasha. They can be seen, with a bit of luck, wherever there is open water. A trip to Red Wing (see page 72), Winona (800-657-4972) or Wabasha (800-565-4158) guarantees a sighting.

BIRD WATCHING

Everyone is born with a bird in their heart.

Frank Chapman
Ornithologist

Some of the best bird watching (birding!) in the Upper Midwest can be found in the Twin Cities. Located at the historic crossroads of three major biomes (northern coniferous forest, eastern deciduous forest and western tallgrass prairie) and blessed with three major river valleys, the metro area provides plentiful habitat for a rich variety of birds. In fact, 340 of the 900 species of birds ever recorded in North America have been seen here.

The winter months are surprisingly good for seeing some of the largest and most spectacular birds. It's not unusual for office workers in downtown St. Paul to look out their window and be startled by the sight of a mature bald eagle gliding over the Mississippi River. Open water along all the major rivers allows these magnificent creatures to spend the winter here. I have seen bald eagles while skiing at half a dozen parks in this book.

Great horned owls are common. During "invasion years" like the winter of 1995–96, great gray owls, boreal owls and snowy owls were seen in several metro locales. Wild turkey populations have been growing rapidly. Rare gulls, trumpeter swans and uncommon waterfowl are possible visitors wherever open water exists. And the 16-inch-high pileated woodpecker resides in most nearby forests.

A great way to kick off the winter bird watching season is to take a trip down to Lake Pepin and the Weaver Marshes to watch the tundra swan migration. By early November, thousands of swans, canvasbacks, mergansers and other waterfowl (along with dozens of eagles) are resting and feeding before their last major push to their wintering grounds. Some of the best viewing is in Wisconsin at Rieck's Lake just north of Alma (608-685-4249) on Highway 35. Many local Audubon clubs make this annual pilgrimage or call the Winona Visitors Bureau at 800-657-4972 for information on their annual **Swan-watch weekend.**

Throughout the winter, open water, pine groves, bird feeders and large undeveloped natural habitat keep a hardy assortment of species around. The cheerful song of the black-capped chickadee can be heard on most any trail. And the Twin Cities occasionally see snowy owls, pine grosbeaks, snow buntings (in flocks on rural roadsides) and other denizens of the far north. Phone the Minnesota Ornithologist's Union (MOU) HOTLINE at 780-8890 for reports of unusual local sightings.

WARNING! Bird watching is perhaps the least aerobic activity in this book. See the WELCOME TO WINTER chapter's section on how to "Dress for Success" and take heed.

GETTING STARTED

The best way to get started is to spend a morning on an organized bird hike led by a skilled guide. All groups welcome beginners and field trips are planned for specific times and locations where birds are likely to be abundant. You will also be able to check out different types of binoculars, spotting scopes and field guides – all essential equipment for good winter birding.

The National Camera Exchange in Golden Valley (546-6831) is one of the best places to buy binoculars and scopes. They publish a small brochure that explains the variety of equipment available.

Roger Tory Peterson's *Eastern Birds* is a good guide for beginners. Experienced birders prefer the more comprehensive *Field Guide to the Birds of North America* published by National Geographic Society. *A Birder's Guide to Minnesota* by Kim Eckert is the most detailed guide to birding locales. Bob Janssen's *Birds in Minnesota* is a comprehensive guide to the distribution of 400 species of birds. The magnificent, two-volume *Birds of Minnesota* by Dr. T. S. Roberts is one of the grandest bird books every published. On the other end of the scale, the *Twin Cities Birding Map* is a handy glove-compartment guide to local viewing spots.

Courtesy of the Raptor Center

A great horned owl tests her wings after being released.

Tundra swans coming in for a landing in early November.

OH, THE PLACES YOU'LL GO!

There is no time like the present to see our national bird, the bald eagle, in the wild. Thanks in large part to a ban on DDT in the 1970s, eagle populations have soared. A census about 25 years ago indicated about 70 nesting pairs in the state. Today there are well over 500 pair, and they have successfully nested at some 20 sites in the seven-county metro area.

I have seen bald eagles in winter at **Afton, Fort Snelling, Frontenac, Kinnickinnick (Wisconsin) and Wild River State Parks**. From an overlook at **Red Wing East End Trails,** I have watched eagles flying 100 feet *below* me.

While it is possible to find eagles on nearly any stretch of open water on the Minnesota, St. Croix or Mississippi Rivers, a day trip down to Winona or Wabasha guarantees a view. On Sunday afternoons, from November through March, the **Wabasha Eagle Watch Observatory** is staffed by volunteers equipped with spotting scopes and information. The March mating season and spring migration bring greater numbers and special programs in the Wabasha (800-565-4158) and Winona (800-657-4972) areas.

OPEN WATER BIRDING

Where you find open water in winter you are sure to find waterfowl, even if you don't happen on an eagle. Mallards, Canada geese, goldeneyes and black ducks are common. Buffleheads, hooded mergansers, pied-billed grebes, wood ducks and widgeons are always possibilities. Check out:

- **Black Dog Lake** is a perennial favorite. Take the 113th St. exit off I-35W in Burnsville and go east on Black Dog Road. The power plant keeps the adjacent lakes open and this area is considered one of the best in the state for rare gulls and winter waterfowl. Phone the Minnesota Valley National Wildlife Refuge at 335-2323 for more information on this and other nearby birding hot spots.

- **Coon Rapids Dam Regional Park** has open water below the dam and trails along both sides of the Mississippi.

- The **King Power Plant** on the St. Croix River (just south of Bayport off Highway 95) has open water that attracts common goldeneye, Barrow's goldeneye (on occasion), gulls and more.

- The **Monticello Nuclear Power Plant** has open water that allowed 167 trumpeter swans to overwinter in 1996. Phone the Lowry Nature Center at 472-4911 for reservations on guided field trips to witness this spectacle.

- **Shepard and Warner Roads** through downtown St. Paul have paths or sidewalks along the Mississippi River. Lilydale Road through **Lilydale Park** is another good eagle-spotting cruise.

The Cannon Valley Trail may be the easiest place around to see wild turkeys. See the trail map (page 36) for specific locations or call 507-263-3954 for current sitings.

Jay Blake

The 16-inch-tall pileated woodpecker is a common winter resident.

UNIQUE PLACES

- The **Wilkie Unit** (page 57) of the Minnesota Valley National Wildlife Refuge (335-2323) is the site of a rare heron rookery with some 600 nests built high in the cottonwood trees. The heron have flown south, but just to the west are the **Blue Lake sewage treatment ponds** where several species of waterfowl can often be seen.

- **Wild River State Park** boasts of seven or eight trumpeter swans that winter on an open stretch of the St. Croix River. The park's bird feeders are quite popular, and flying squirrels even inhabit the park. Unfortunately, they're nocturnal.

- The **Isaac Walton League Headquarters** at 6601 Auto Club Road in Bloomington (944-1423) has conifer groves where both saw-whet and long-eared owls are winter visitors.

- Sure, you can see trumpeter swans in the aerated pond at the **Minnesota Zoo**, but sneak inside the Tropics Trail Building and scope out the wild assortment of free-flying tropical birds.

BIRD FEEDERS

Many regional and state parks in the metro area have nature or visitors' centers with an array of bird feeders. Guaranteed visitors include black-capped chickadees, blue jays, nuthatches, goldfinches, cardinals, tree sparrows, pine siskins and four species of woodpeckers. Grosbeaks, finches and redpolls are also possible.

Of course, many winter birdwatchers never leave their kitchen. (See what you've been missing!) *Wild About Birds: The DNR Bird Feeding Guide* by Carrol Henderson is the best book ever written on setting up your own wildlife refuge.

BIRDING ORGANIZATIONS AND EVENTS

Minnesota Ornithologists Union
HOTLINE 780-8890

Begun in 1938, the MOU is an outstanding statewide organization for both amateurs and professionals. The HOTLINE is updated weekly (at least) with sightings and locations of rare or notable birds. Members receive *The Loon* quarterly and the MOU newsletter bimonthly.

Audubon Society, Minnesota Office
Phone 225-1830

There are five local chapters, and national membership automatically enlists you with the closest one. The St. Paul Chapter (291-2596), Minneapolis, Roseville Bird Club, Upper Hiawatha Valley (Red Wing) and Minnesota River Valley Clubs all sponsor an annual **Christmas Bird Count.** This tradition began in 1900, and Twin Cities chapters typically record 45 to 50 species, with several thousand individual birds sighted during the day-long outing.

Bell Museum of Natural History
Phone 624-7083

The University of Minnesota's Bell Museum is an excellent resource, with nationally renowned wildlife dioramas by Francis Lee Jacques. Bruce Fall leads some of the best local birding field trips around, and the Blue Heron Bookshop carries the area's largest selection of bird books.

Hennepin Parks
Phone 559-9000

Leaders in local conservation efforts, such as the trumpeter swan and bluebird recovery programs. Their nature centers offer bird banding programs and birding hikes every month of the year.

Raptor Center
Phone 624-4745

A leading research and rehabilitation center for hawks, eagles and owls. Call ahead for tours of the facility (the closest you can get to a live eagle) or dates of their semi-annual bird release programs.

Wildlife Rehabilitation Clinic
Phone 624-7730

The clinic is open seven days a week and takes all injured or orphaned wild animals or birds except raptors.

Courtesy of the Minnesota Zoo

Trumpeter swans enjoying a splash at the Minnesota Zoo.

Skate skiers and classic striders share the trail with a smile at Baker Park Reserve.

CROSS COUNTRY SKIING

*N*othing makes the body so strong and elastic ... nothing gives better presence and freshens the mind as cross country skiing. It is something that develops not only the body but also the soul.

Fridtjof Nansen, Norwegian Arctic Explorer

Cross country skiing in the Twin Cities metropolitan area is as good as you'll find anywhere on the planet. There are over 900 kilometers (550 miles!) of ski trails described and mapped in this book. You can ski through flat and open fields of prairie, or whistle down narrow trails lined with pine trees.

In the Twin Cities metro area, there is enough snow for skiing from early December through mid-March. Sometimes it may require a bit of traveling to find good snow. There are one dozen day trips described here and *over the last several years you could always find enough snow to ski somewhere in the area on any given winter day*. A depressing rain in Eagan could easily bring several inches of fresh snow to Wild River State Park near North Branch.

Modern grooming equipment does an amazing job of rejuvenating old, crusty snow after thaws and even rain. Most parks have good grooming, but **Hennepin Parks** (559-9000) is the local master. I have enjoyed great skiing at Hyland and Baker Park Reserve *weeks* after the last decent snowfall. Of course, if you are a skate skier you may even look forward to hardpacked, near icy conditions. With a good edge you can darn near fly.

Cross country skiing is great fun, as well as great exercise. Everyone who lives here should learn the basics so they can take part. Learn-to-ski programs are available at the bigger park systems. Or, join the **North Star Ski Touring Club** (924-9922), **Sierra Club** (379-3853) or **Minnesota Rovers** (257-7324) for camaraderie, ski trips and more.

Petroglyph of a skier found in Rodoy, Norway.

HISTORY OF CROSS COUNTRY SKIING

The petroglyph, or stone carving, shown above is the earliest known image of an individual on skis. It was found in northern Norway at Rodoy, and dates back some 7,000 years. The oldest ski is from 2,500 B.C. It was preserved in a bog near Hoting, Norway.

There are no accounts, to my knowledge, of the Ojibwa or Dakota using skis for winter travel. The Ojibwa used snowshoes. The first reported use of skis for cross country travel in Minnesota dates back to before Minnesota's statehood. In 1853, a Norwegian skier with "strips of smooth wood, about six feet long and three inches wide and turned up like sleigh runners in front," traveled to St. Paul from Lake Superior. This predates the famous mountain mail deliveries of John "Snowshoe" (they were really skis) Thompson by about three years. From those early pioneer days throughout the 1800s skis were used in Minnesota for delivering mail, collecting taxes, grocery shopping, visiting friends and even pallbearing a coffin.

With its long Scandinavian heritage, it is natural that skiing was not an uncommon form of winter travel in the metro area. But what is fascinating are the direct links that Minnesota has with the birth of modern sport skiing in northern Europe and St. Paul's place in history as the site of the country's first organized ski club and first governed cross country "ski run" and ski jumping competition.

The following information was gathered in part from two outstanding publications, *The Tale of a Comet and Other Stories* by Helen White and *Nine Thousand Years of Skis* by Ted Bays. Recent history was gathered from the North Star Ski Touring Club and other sources. See the SKI JUMPING chapter for more local ski history.

Collection of Rudi Hargesheimer

Cross country skiing for transportation and, we imagine, recreation goes back several thousand years, but its history as a sport has roots in the Norwegian military. As early as 960 A.D., ski running was part of every "highborn" soldier's training. In 1206, during the Norwegian civil war, Viking soldiers nicknamed "Birkebeiners" for the birchbark leggings they wore, rescued the child prince Haakon Haakonsson by skiing 55 kilometers to safety. North America's largest cross country ski race, the American Birkebeiner, commemorates this. (See the "Ski Events" section.)

In 1767, the Norwegian military held its first cross country ski racing competition. The first competitions open to civilians were held in Tromsoy, Norway, in 1843 and included both ski jumping and ski running. By 1850, a 25-year-old skier from Morgedal in Telemark decided that to take full advantage of his skis they must be more firmly attached to his boots. Some 7,000 years after the first ski was toe-strapped on, Sondre Norheim devised an osier (willow twig) binding that would wrap around his heel and hold it in place.

An osier binding from Varmland, Sweden.

The modern sport of skiing was born.

Norheim had created the binding that would change the face of ski jumping, allow the first controlled "Telemark" turns and invent the slalom downhill style still used today. Sondre Norheim *skied* to his watershed 1868 ski jumping competition in Christiana (present-day Oslo). And, in 1884, Sondre Norheim emigrated with his family to Minnesota, where he settled in Oslo in the Red River Valley.

Two of Norheim's best pupils from Telemark would shortly follow him over. Mikkel Hemmestvedt had won several King's Cups in Norway for long-distance skiing and ski jumping when he moved to the prairies of Norman County, Minnesota, in 1886. In a similar fashion, Mikkel's brother Torjus won the first 50 kilometer race in Huseby, Norway, in 1888 and moved to Minnesota later that year.

Their arrival coincided with the first ski competitions to be held as part of the newly celebrated St. Paul Winter Carnival. The 1886 ski competition had been cancelled due to a thaw, but when Mikkel and his Norman County friends heard that a $100 prize was being offered as part of the second winter carnival's ski tournament, they quickly formed a ski club and took the train down to St. Paul.

The Scandinavian Ski Club of St. Paul hosted the first governed ski tournament to be held in the U.S. on January 25, 1887. Eight clubs with some 80 members altogether, participated in the all-day tournament that featured — besides the competition — a downtown parade and banquet with speeches on patriotism and the noble virtues of skiing, plus music and dancing into the night.

Mikkel won the first-class competition with a 60-foot leap and took the mile ski run in four and a half minutes, topping his closest rival by more than a minute. Later he gave a ski exhibition near today's State Capital grounds and was invited to join both the St. Paul and St. Croix Falls, Wisconsin, ski clubs.

Mikkel left for Wisconsin and joined two fellow Norwegians in forming the Excelsior Ski Company in St. Croix Falls. The pine Telemark skis were manufactured to Mikkel's design and specifications. They were perhaps the first commercially-made skis in America.

By 1890, both Mikkel and his brother Torjus had moved to Red Wing, Minnesota, where they joined the Aurora Club and worked at the Red Wing Furniture Company making skis after work. The Aurora Club was one of the Midwest's strongest. They held practice runs weekly and cross country excursions of 30 to 40 miles when snow and weather permitted.

In 1907, the Dayton's Bluff Ski Club for youth formed. The St. Paul Ski Club's annual report recorded a cross country ski run to Red Rock (Newport, northeast corner of Bailey Road and Highway 61) on March 3 that "was perfectly enchanting. The fresh snow covered all roads and old tracks. Everything gave us the feeling of pioneers in an unknown country where human feet had never trodden."

St. Paul Ski Club member Julius Blegen won the three-and-a-half mile cross country competition with a time of 23 minutes, 20 seconds at the 1912 National Ski Tournament. At the 1917 Winter Carnival, a ski race from Fort Snelling to Dunning Field was one of the largest events. In 1923, Sigurd Overby from the St. Paul Ski Club

From left: Paul Honningstad, Mikkel and Torjus Hemmestvedt and B.L. Hjermstad – Aurora Ski Club members in 1890.

NORTHLAND SKIS

Christian Lund came to St. Paul from Oslo, Norway, and began the Northland Ski Company in 1911. For many years it was billed as "the largest manufacturer of skis in the world."

won the National Cross Country Championship with a time of 38 minutes, five seconds on the seven-mile course. He was the top U.S. representative at the first Winter Olympics, held in 1924 in Chamonix, France.

Norm Oakvik, a Norwegian of course, is the man who bridged the era from when any skier worth their salt was able to ski jump, slalom and go cross country ski running — to the present era of specialized athletes, one-piece lycra outfits and groomed ski trails. Norm's father, who was a ski jumper in Norway, made him a pair of jumping skis at the age of 11 or 12. He participated in the ski racing program at North High School and in the 1940s became a member of the Minneapolis Ski Club. He raced for a while and won the National Nordic Combined (ski jumping and cross country) Championship and the North American Special Cross Country Championship.

Norm   *Jinny*

Jinny McWethy met Norm Oakvik around 1960 and he got her going on the skinny skis. In 1965, the United States Ski Association (USSA), which already included cross country ski racing, wanted to expand into ski touring and invited Norm to chair a committee. He gathered together Jinny, Bob Larson and a couple of others, and they took four or five trips around the Twin Cities.

In 1966, Bob Larson took over the committee that included Norm, Jinny, Dwight Johnson, Shirley Esnough, Lon Wiedenhaft and Dag Helgestad. A two-mile cross country ski trail was cut near the Bush Lake ski jump. While a few high school teams still had training loops, this was one of the very first recreational trails.

Cross country skiing had fallen so far out of the public eye that in 1966–67 the only place in town to buy skis was from Norm Oakvik. In fact, Hoigaards bought their first skis from Norm that winter — two pair. But cross country skiing was about to rise again, championed by folks like Ralph Thornton and Ben Kern of the *Minneapolis Star and Tribune* and State Senator Henry McKnight, whose land at Jonathan, Minnesota, would soon become the local ski touring center.

In the summer of 1967, the North Star Ski Touring Club (NSSTC) was officially born at a meeting at Dwight Johnson's house. Lon Weidenhaft was elected the first club president and there were 19 charter members. Trips that winter included perennial favorites like Wirth Park and Bush Lake, plus distant memories such as Gridley's Tree Farm and El Rancho Mañana.

Interest in cross country skiing was starting to awaken, as Wayne Lindskoog wrote, "like a sleeping giant beneath the snow." The winter of 1970–71 was pivotal. Nearly 1,000 people crowded into the first general NSSTC meeting. The first "modern" ski tour/race took place in February 1971. About 300 skiers took part in the Victoria-Jonathan-Carver (VJC) race, and Tim Heisel took home the first Jonathan Cup. He won the next two Jonathan Cups as well.

The demand for dedicated and maintained ski trails was just beginning. Club president Glen Bennington and Tim Knopp wrote a letter to the Hennepin County Park Reserve District (HCPRD, now Hennepin Parks) to impress this upon them. HCPRD took notice and began to build the region's most extensive and best-maintained ski trail system.

The NSSTC club newsletter, *Loype,* was first issued in July 1971. *Loype,* according to resident linguist Wayne Lindskoog, means "kindly remove yourself from the place in which I am about to ski." Norwegian traditionalists prefer to translate *Loype* as "track" or "ski trail."

Tim Knopp and the North Star Ski Touring Club published the first regional guide to cross country skiing in 1971. The booklet included 23 Minnesota areas and eight more in Michigan, Wisconsin and Canada. Only a handful of these areas had maintained ski trails and some were open only to groups.

As Tim explained in his introduction to the third edition of *Ski Minnesota,* local and state park agencies had not yet recognized the need for dedicated, maintained ski trails. Why did skiers need trails when they could go anywhere? Truth was that they were being forced to beat through the bush or compete with snowmobiles. Fortunately, the Hennepin County Park Reserve District had just completed their acquisition phase and embraced cross country skiing. The trails they created became wildly successful and led the way for other state and local agencies.

To foster this development, Tim Knopp and Jack Maloney wrote the *Ski Touring Trail Planner* (1973) and helped form the Minnesota Federation of Ski Touring Clubs (Minntour, 1972). Serving as a collective voice for the needs of cross country skiers to land management agencies, Minntour sponsored trail development seminars and was instrumental in the fight to reclaim and preserve the BWCA wilderness.

In February 1972, the first Marine-on-St. Croix Race was held at William O'Brien State Park. Good snow, bad snow or (almost) no snow, this race has been held every year since and is now billed as the "longest continuously run ski race in North America." William O'Brien was one of the first state parks to complete a trail system in 1974 and it remains one of the most popular.

Through pure coincidence, two ski marathon races that were first held in February 1973 are now the largest in North America. On February 24th, 54 skiers lined up to run the first American Birkebeiner. North Star Jacque Lindskoog was the only woman of the 35 who completed the full 48-kilometer course from Hayward to the Telemark Lodge in Wisconsin. Meanwhile, on February 25, in Mora, Minnesota, the first Mora Vasaloppet was held. Both events commemorate historic Northern European events and are more fully described in the "Ski Events" section.

Will Steger was a North Star in 1975, and Jinny McWethy recalled him joining a trip to Olympia Village, Wisconsin, and bringing with him "huge heavy skis and a ton of army surplus clothes." Perhaps he was already thinking toward the ski and dog sled trips that would take him to the North Pole (on May 1, 1986) and 3,741 miles across the Antarctica (July 27, 1989 to March 3, 1990).

Bill Koch won a silver medal in cross country ski racing at the 1976 Winter Olympics and the sport took off. The mid-1970s saw a great surge of public participation plus the introduction of new synthetic clothing and equipment that would compete with wool and woodies for the hearts and minds of cross country skiers everywhere. One old quote read, "If God had meant us to ski on fiberglass skis, he would have made fiberglass trees!"

The historic start of the first Birkebeiner race that began in front of the Lumberjack Bowl Pancake House on February 24, 1973.

Courtesy of the American Birkebeiner

The need for dedicated funding for cross country ski trails became clear in 1982 when snowmobilers obtained exclusive rights to all unrefunded gas tax dollars. To counteract this development, the Minnesota Ski Pass Program was launched for the 1983–84 season. The pass generated $161,000 its first year and remains an important tool for statewide and local ski trail development.

The mid-1980s began another time of transition as skate skiing techniques began to dominate competition on the local, national and international levels. Ahvo Taipale was born near Jyväskylä, Finland, and moved to the Twin Cities in 1974. He won many local races and began teaching and coaching the latest training and racing techniques. In 1985 and 1986, he co-wrote two booklets — *Improve Your Skiing* and *The Finnish Ski Training System* — that illustrated and described the new ski skating technique. Ahvo is a firm believer in the classical style as well and continues to spread the gospel of nordic skiing from his shop, Finn Sisu Sports, in St. Paul.

While skate skiing appeared to be the next big thing, the truth is that the technique has been used in one form or another for decades. *Learn to Ski,* published in 1935, has a chapter, "Skating on Skis," that discusses the advantage this technique offers on slightly downhill grades.

Hennepin Parks was again a leader in recognizing and accommodating the need for skate skiing lanes as part of its trail system. In the winter of 1986–87, they added skating trails to eight regional parks and joined the Minneapolis Ski Club and Midwest Mountaineering in offering skating clinics. That winter also ushered in the first lighted ski trail at Hyland Lake Park Reserve.

Today there are more choices and opportunities for a superior cross country skiing experience than ever before. Grooming techniques and equipment (the first Birkebeiner was tracked by two youngsters, one driving a snowmobile pulling the other on alpine skis) are vastly improved and can generate a good surface even after thaws and rain. Modern synthetic clothing (and good old wool) make it easy to stay warm and comfortable outdoors.

The bigger question is societal. In a consumer-driven, entertainment-oriented age where lifestyles are purchased and every step is climate-controlled, is there still a place for outside exercise and communing with winter? When people push away the screen, will they walk over to their cross country ski exercise machine or step out the door, find their place in the sun and reel off a few rhythmic kilometers?

Perhaps it will be the difference between the easy life and the good life.

William O'Brien, one of the first metro cross country ski centers.

Ahvo Taipale skate skiing a trail.

DRESS FOR SUCCESS

*P*erfect! — 20 or 30 below zero.

Will Steger, on being asked what the weather was like on a 5,000-mile dog sled and ski trip from Duluth to Alaska.

See the WELCOME TO WINTER chapter for a complete look at dressing to stay warm and dry. The wicking layer is especially critical for cross country skiers. When skiing, **gaiters or anklets** are a must to protect the socks and ankle area. **Overboots** are a welcome addition when the temperature drops below zero. Moving your toes when you're stopped is a trick I recall from my downhill days.

DON'T LEAVE HOME WITHOUT IT

Pack the following in a fanny or day pack so it's ready when you are. Then just fill up the water bottles, add snacks and go. You'll be happier if you've eaten (carbohydrates!) and had your fill of water or juices before leaving. Coffee (like alcohol) tends to dehydrate the body, but a hot mug for the road sure tastes great.

- Skis, boots, poles and wax
- Map and compass – skills to use
- Water bottle(s) – filled
- Wool cap or poly balaclava (wrap water bottle)
- Mittens, extra wool socks
- Lip balm (Carmex), skin protector
- Handkerchief, paper towels
- Snacks – gorp, fruit, cheese, sausage, hard candy
- Plastic bag to carry out waste – yours and others
- Watch – check time when leaving and halfway out
- Camera and film
- **Minnesota Ski Pass**
- Sun glasses, sunscreen
- Pocket knife
- Flashlight, stick matches or lighter

Additional items for longer outings or when leading a group:

- **Lunch!** If you're stopping for more than a couple minutes, the first thing everyone should do is pull out the extra parka or sweater (it's probably next to the food) and put it on *before* people start cooling off. A thermos filled with hot soup or chili, deli sandwiches, smoked fish, brownies, cookies, fine cheeses, bread and hard candy all taste great on the trail. Bring a plastic tablecloth (space blanket) pad(s) to sit on, utensils, paper towels and garbage bag.

- **Ski repair stuff** – ski tip, scraper, duct tape, binding, screws, tools, 1/8" nylon line, pocket knife

- **First aid kit** – zip lock bag (when filled with snow it doubles as an ice pack for sprains) with aspirin, ace bandage, moleskin, matches, bandages, heat compress (for frost bite), 2 large garbage bags (to use as emergency blanket or sleeping bag) or a space blanket, whistle (3 long then 3 short whistles means SOS).

RECOGNIZING HYPOTHERMIA — Frostbite, page 10

Hypothermia is the number one killer of people recreating outdoors. It can even happen in relatively mild weather with the temperature between 30 and 50 degrees. It results when body heat is lost faster than the body's metabolism can replace it and a person's body core temperature drops.

Shivering, slurred speech, clumsiness or difficulty walking or skiing are indications that a person may be developing hypothermia. Dressing properly, keeping dry, eating right and drinking plenty of fluids goes a long way in preventing hypothermia. **Never ignore shivering!** If you feel that you or someone else is "going hypothermic" you must act *immediately* to:

- Get out of the cold to a dry, warm shelter
- Reduce heat loss by removing wet clothing and adding dry clothing, getting into a sleeping bag if possible, etc.
- Drink warm, high-calorie fluids
- **Seek medical attention!**

THE GREAT MINNESOTA SKI PASS

The Minnesota Ski Pass is required by law on most public ski trails. To order, phone 296-6157 weekdays. They take credit cards.

Courtesy of Hennepin Parks

*Groups and families go at the rate of the slowest skier. Make it fun and not too long for kids. Call the **Minnesota Youth Ski League** at 487-6714 to get your kids started on the right foot.*

SKI TOURING IN COMFORT

1. Choosing a trail is half the fun. Pick a ski trail that everybody agrees on and is within everybody's ability level.

> *Warming House (Visitor Center, etc.) as shown on the following ski trail maps.*

Trails described as groomed in this book are maintained by machines that can recondition crusty or icy snow and lay a fresh track. Trails that are simply trackset get icy sooner. Follow these guidelines:

● **Easier or Beginner** The trail is flat to gently rolling. Bring the family.

〽 **More difficult or Intermediate** These trails start to roll in places and often require the ability to herringbone up a moderate incline. Ability to snowplow may be necessary when descending a hill. Not appropriate for first-time skiers.

◆ **Most difficult, Advanced or Expert** Experienced skiers seek these places out for their challenge and excitement. The ability to climb steep hills and negotiate fast, curving downhills (even when icy) is essential.

2. Decide before you leave when you want to be back or if you'll stop to eat on your way home. Add some extra travel time if the trail is new for you.

3. Use the following travel times when choosing a trail. Lunch stops are extra. Trail lengths are generally given in kilometers in this book because of the Scandinavian origins of the sport and because it sounds like you covered more ground.

One Kilometer (3,280 feet) equals 5/8 of a mile
One mile (5,280 feet) equals 1.6 kilometers

Beginners – 1.5 to 3 kilometers per hour
Intermediate recreational skiers – 3 to 6 kilometers per hour
Experts, skate skiers – 8 to 25 kilometers per hour

4. Will Steger has two pieces of advice on venturing out in the cold. Dress properly and **eat right**. You wouldn't insulate a house that isn't heated so it follows that the well-dressed skier needs a good meal before hitting the trail. You have to "fuel the fire," is how Steger puts it.

The best type of meal is one that is loaded with carbohydrates and fat rather than protein. A big bowl of oatmeal and butter works great. Racers eat two or three hours beforehand or enjoy a big meal of pasta the night before skiing.

Courtesy of Hennepin Parks

Pick a trail that everyone agrees on and ski at your own pace. Preplan rendezvous points.

5. At the trailhead, stretch and warm-up the muscles.

6. Make sure the lights on your car are off, keys are in a zippered pocket and that everybody has a map and knows the general plan.

7. Ski at your own pace and pick a couple rendezvous points where you can regroup – for lunch or at a scenic overlook. Stop immediately if you need to add or remove clothing, eat or drink. You can catch up with the group later.

8. Know your ability. Don't ski down a hill you don't like just because someone else did. Walk down and be happy.

9. Drink plenty of water before and during your tour. You sweat (and dehydrate) just as much in winter as in summer. People underestimate how dried out they get because the air is bone dry.

10. Eat frequent snacks and drink before you are thirsty.

11. Watch the weather and your progress on the trail. Groups go as fast as the slowest member. Turning back early beats getting lost in the dark.

12. When loading and unloading cars, place things on the front hood. This lessens the chance that they'll be forgotten, left behind or run over.

GETTING STARTED

> *For the things we have to learn*
> *before we can do them,*
> *we learn by doing them.*
> **Aristotle**

There is nothing so natural as the rhythm of cross country skiing.

KICK *glide* . . . KICK *glide* . . . KICK *glide* . . .

The cadence sets in, thoughts drift away and the countryside rolls by. While running a mile seems like hard work, skiing all afternoon is mostly pure fun.

For those just beginning, it helps to take a lesson, get a few words of encouragement and get out in the woods. Keep it simple but get a few pointers. Parents with kids will appreciate the **Minnesota Youth Ski League** (487-6714), a noncompetitive program for children ages four to fifteen. They make skiing fun, a game.

Hennepin Parks (559-9000), **Midwest Mountaineering** (339-3433) and **Finn Sisu Sports** (645-2443) are good places to find out about lessons. The **North Star Ski Touring Club** (924-9922) sponsors dozens of ski trips for all levels of skiers each winter. **Gear West** (473-0093) is great for learning about racing.

You need to visualize good technique and then practice it. They used to say, "if you can walk, you can ski." But walking on skis is not skiing. (Walking on snowshoes *is* snowshoeing though, so skip ahead if you must.) To ski you must learn how to KICK and *glide*.

You are actually gliding on a very thin layer of water caused by the ski's friction. The moment the ski stops moving that water refreezes. That brief grip of ski frozen to snow allows the skier to "kick" forward without slipping. Try it!

Good no-wax skis are now light enough and fast enough that it makes sense to rent or even buy them for starters. They are super convenient and even experienced skiers will keep a pair on hand for spring skiing when no-wax skis simply fly through wet and near icy snow.

Waxable skis are faster than waxless and when temperatures remain under 25° require just a single type of wax. Today's touring equipment performs far better than wood skis and three-pin bindings.

SKATING WITH SKIS

When skate skiing first appeared on the European racing circuit it changed everything. It is simply a faster and more efficient skiing technique. In the past 15 years, skate skiing has become widely accepted by recreational skiers as well. In fact, very short skating skis are now being marketed to the vast numbers of in-line skaters because the technique is similar. Nearly half of the ski trails in this book have parallel tracks for skate skiing.

Some thoughts on skate skiing:

- It's another way to enjoy skiing and is relatively easy to learn.

- In low snow years you will still be able to ski almost every day. Packed snow, thin snow, even near icy conditions can be skated.

- Skating increases the variety of places you can ski — lakes, rivers, old railroad beds, even snowmobile trails are new-found paradises.

Herringbone step up a hill.

Snowplow to go slow downhill.

Northland Ski Catalog

As you fall — relax — and sit down. Do not try to catch yourself. Get on your knees to get back up.

Drawing by Abbott Rosenthal

COME AND LIGHT YOUR CANNON!

THE
2ND ANNUAL
CANNONBALL RACES.

ANNUAL SKI EVENTS

The following list includes competitive races that have some history. Check clubs and stores each year for a complete schedule. *Silent Sports* magazine (715-258-5546) publishes an excellent regional calendar in their monthly magazine.

WINTERFEST
Two weekends before Thanksgiving
Sponsored by Midwest Mountaineering (339-3433), this is a great event for learning about the latest in equipment, techniques and places to go.

FINN SISU PHALEN HIHTO/GRAND PRIX RACE
New Year's Eve/New Year's Day
Phalen Regional Park, phone 266-6445
Hihto means cross country ski race in Finnish. Co-sponsored by the St. Paul Parks Division — separate men's and women's starts.

TWIN CITIES CHAMPIONSHIPS
Early January weekend
Locations vary, phone 424-2017
Sponsored by the Minneapolis Ski Club (943-8956), this two-day event features 10 kilometer classical races on Saturday and freestyle races on Sunday — there are women's, men's and youth divisions.

LA LA PALOOZA LOPPET
Later in January
Como Park, phone 266-6445
A 13-kilometer race with separate starts for men and women.

KING BOREAS SKI RACE
Winter Carnival (late January - early February)
Phalen-Keller Regional Park, 266-6445
First run in 1971, this 15-kilometer freestyle race has a reputation as one of the rowdier cross country ski events.

BAKER SHAKER
Last Saturday in January
Baker Park Reserve, phone 559-6700
One of the oldest local citizen's races. There is a 10-kilometer morning race with a 2-kilometer (or less) kid's race at noon.

CANNONBALL RACES
First Saturday in February
Cannon Falls Scout Camp, phone 224-1891, ext. 154
This benefit for the Boy Scouts of America has several categories — from a 1-kilometer kid's race (free!) to a 42-kilometer freestyle race. This is a once-a-year opportunity to ski the private and quite scenic trails at the camp on Lake Byllesby.

MARINE-ON-ST. CROIX SKI RACE
First Sunday in February
William O'Brien State Park, phone 433-0500
Billed as the "oldest continually run ski race in North America," this event began in 1972 and uses scenic state park trails for its course.

MORA VASALOPPET
Second Sunday in February
Mora, Minnesota, phone 800-368-6672
The race begins with a bang. A stick of dynamite goes off and so do the skiers. The Mora Vasaloppet is America's second largest citizen ski race and features lengths from 13 kilometers up to the premier 58-kilometer marathon. The 2,500 plus participants include some of the sport's top racers. After a tour of the surrounding countryside, the racers sprint down Main Street to the finish line.

The Mora Vasaloppet offers some intriguing side events like the **Lantern Loppet** night tour and the **Mora Minniloppet** for kids, held on Saturday. Mora is small-town Minnesota at its best. The locals make blueberry soup for the rest stops, and a big pasta dinner is held the night before the race. The Mora Vasaloppet is based on the Swedish Vasaloppet that began in 1922. It is the world's oldest cross country ski marathon and is based on the flight of Gustav Vasa by ski who, after initially being spurned, came back to lead the rebellion against the Danes who were occupying their country.

AMERICAN BIRKEBEINER
Saturday later in February
Cable to Hayward, WI, phone 800-872-2753
On February 24, 1973, 35 skiers lined up for the first American Birkebeiner (19 more skied the shorter korteloppet). The 25th anniversary in 1997 will see some 8,000 skiers surging forward in a human tidal wave at the biggest ski event in North America.

The Birkie is the granddaddy of American ski races and the only U.S. race in the fabled world loppet series. The original Norwegian Birkebeiner-Rennet race began in 1932 to commemorate the epic journey of the "Birch Legs." In 1206, two Birkebeiner soldiers, with their birch-bark leggings, skied 55 kilometers to rescue the 2-year-old Prince Hakon Hakonsson. Nowadays, 2-year-olds – or at least 3-year-olds — can take part in the **Barnebirkie** race on Thursday before the big race. Nearly 2,000 children from 3 to 13 participate.

CROSS COUNTRY SKI CLUBS

There are several local clubs that run trips for every interest and budget. Many trips are free with club membership.

Minneapolis Ski Club

Mark Lahtinen, Cross Country Skiing Chair, 424-2017

Jack Broz, 943-8956

The Minneapolis Ski Club is the area's premier racing club. The club has had members competing at the Olympics for decades and several of these national-caliber athletes have stayed on to coach. There are 400 to 500 members who participate in all aspects of nordic competition and training for juniors and adults (See SKI JUMPING chapter).

Minnesota Rovers Outing Club

P.O. Box 14133

Minneapolis, MN 55414

HOTLINE 257-7324

Organized in 1954, Rovers is one of the oldest outdoor adventure clubs in the Midwest. They have a strong emphasis on tripping and draw a wide range of members from University students to those on the far side of forty. Skiing, snowshoeing and winter camping.

Minnesota Ski Council (MSC)

P.O. Box 4063

St. Paul, MN 55104

An umbrella group that publishes the *MSC Club Roster* with information on several Twin Cities ski clubs. Many clubs, like the **Sitzmark Ski Club** (545-1151), offer downhill and cross country ski trips.

Minnesota Youth Ski League

P.O. Box 14132

St. Paul, MN 55114

Phone 487-6714

A terrific volunteer organization that helps get kids from 4 to 15 excited about cross country skiing. The emphasis is on noncompetitive activities based on Laurie Gullion's seminal book, *Ski Games.*

North Star Ski Touring Club

P.O. Box 4275

St. Paul, MN 55104

HOTLINE 924-9922

The club has some 2,000 members (including a singles division) and a very active trip schedule that lasts from November into April and travels from just out the back door to the back country of Norway. Members receive the excellent *Loype* newsletter. The club is active year-round with biking, hiking and canoeing.

Sierra Club

Phone 379-3853

A nonprofit, environmental conservation organization with an active singles group, the *Sierran Adventurers.*

Ski For Light

Phone 827-3232

Founded in 1975 to promote physical fitness and social well-being for adults who are visually and mobility impaired. People with and without disabilities join together to learn outdoor activities in one-to-one relationships. Many have gone on to ski the Birkie together.

FRED'S BEST CROSS COUNTRY SKI AREAS

Here's my top baker's dozen in alphabetical order. If the list gravitates to the south and east, well, that's where the hills and dales are. Most of these parks have trails for all skiing abilities. See maps and descriptions for more details.

1. **Afton State Park** – day or night, Afton's a winner.

2. **Battle Creek Regional Park** – the Winthrop site is fine and the future looks bright for lit ski trails.

3. **Cottage Grove Ravine Regional Park** – an almost perfect mix of steep hills and striding areas, evergreens and oaks.

4. **Elk River Ski Trails** – best local area you've never heard of.

5. **French Regional Park** – the night time is the right time.

6. **Hoffman Hills State Park** – a great day trip with big hills.

7. **Lebanon Hills Regional Park** – three places in one, with plenty of terrain for all.

8. **Louisville Swamp** – a vast land resonating with history. Easier trails in a remote setting.

9. **Mille Lacs Kathio State Park** – a huge park with good hills, snowshoe treks, sledding and American Indian history.

10. **Red Wing East End Trails** – blufftop skiing where eagles dare.

11. **Spring Lake Regional Park** – a rolling panorama of the Mighty Mississippi for beginners, families and friends.

12. **Sunfish Lake Park** – a city park with regional appeal.

13. **Wirth Park** – skyline views in the late afternoon sun, plus expert single-track trails near the tamarack bog.

 Warming House (Visitor Center, etc.) as shown on the following ski trail maps.

FLY BY NIGHT SKIING

About every other park in this book has one full moon or candlelight ski outing each winter. Many of the trails in this book are open at night. State parks are open until 10 p.m., and both **Afton** (with light spilling over from the downhill area) and **Fort Snelling** (the flat Pike Island loop) are worth exploring in the light of a full moon.

The Twin Cities are ripe for a cross country ski facility that has snowmaking, a handsome chalet with good food and warmly lit ski trails. **French Regional Park** has much of the above but lacks snowmaking and, ideally, a first-rate restaurant. As it is, they will draw 450 people on a weekday night with good snow. **Wirth Park** is open until 9 p.m. and has a friendly, Swiss-style chalet with refreshments.

Both **Como Park** and **Phalen Regional Park** are reasonably well-lit and do a good business at night. Snowmaking at Como has been discussed. **Hyland Lake Park Reserve** and **Elm Creek Park Reserve** will have lit 5-kilometer ski trails beginning in 1998.

AFTON STATE PARK

Administered by Minnesota DNR   Phone 436-5391

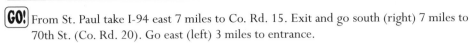

GO! From St. Paul take I-94 east 7 miles to Co. Rd. 15. Exit and go south (right) 7 miles to 70th St. (Co. Rd. 20). Go east (left) 3 miles to entrance.

Trackset 32 km (20 mi)   **Rating** Plenty of terrain for everyone. Great downhill ravine runs.

Fee $4 two-day, $20 annual pass, MN Ski Pass   **Hours** 8 a.m. to 10 p.m. except registered campers

Warming House 9 a.m. to 4 p.m. daily   **Toilet** Indoors 24 hours   **Size** 1,540 acres

Snowshoeing Anywhere but ski trails   **Camping** Ski-in 1 mile, $7 per night, sites 3, 5 and 8 have vistas.

Afton has it all for the classical skier. A terrific network of challenging trails, scenic overlooks and watchable wildlife. You'll like it so much you'll want to spend the night.

Afton takes its name from the nearby village platted in May, 1855. C. S. Gretchell adopted it from the poem *Afton Water* by Robert Burns who sang about the "neighboring hills and clear winding rills." Rills being streams, and none finer than Trout Brook that runs through the park.

The park owes its existence to the efforts of Chester Wilson and the underrated Minnesota Parks and Trails Council. Afton State Park was established in 1969 to preserve and perpetuate the natural landscape features of the St. Croix River Valley. The broad waters of the St. Croix River follow the park for 2 1/2 miles. There are six designated overlooks along the trails that provide great vistas over the river and fine spots for a picnic.

The ski trails follow the narrow wooded ravines from river's edge to the blufftops crowned with native prairie planting and oak savanna. The 300 feet of elevation change allows for some exhilarating downhill runs. While most of these can be handled by a skilled intermediate skier, those marked "dangerous" are for experts only, and even these will be closed when conditions are icy.

Deep in the park there are cedar glades, hardwood forests and a surprising and dramatic rock outcropping along Trout Brook. Wildlife is plentiful and you are almost guaranteed to see deer here if you spend any time at all. Bird life in winter is also abundant, and by March hawks and eagles are soaring above open stretches of the St. Croix. If you are lucky you may also spot pileated woodpeckers, juncos, snow buntings or cedar waxwings.

This is a popular place for full moon skiing, augmented on some trails by the light spilling over from the Afton Alps downhill ski area. At least one official candlelight ski takes place near the time of a full moon.

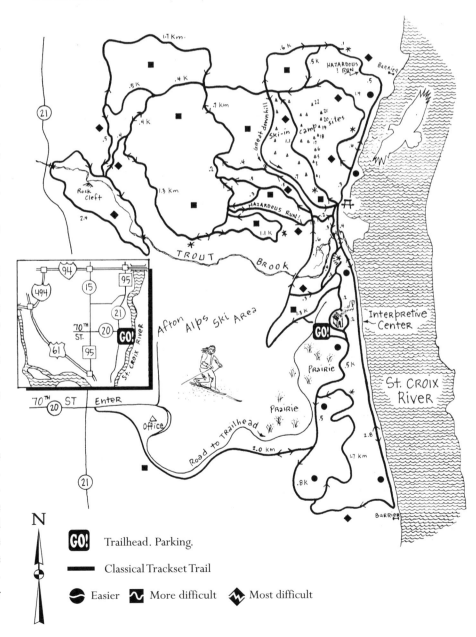

N

GO!   Trailhead. Parking.

————   Classical Trackset Trail

⬤ Easier   〰 More difficult   ◆ Most difficult

2 ANOKA COUNTY SKI TRAILS

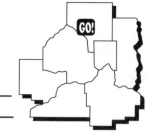

Administered by Anoka County   Phone 767-2870   Hotline 767-2820

Fee Free, MN Ski Pass required   **Hours** Sunrise to 9:30 p.m.

Grooming Trails have tracks set with new snow but are not groomed.

*S*outhern Anoka County has three ski areas, each with its own unique setting. Enjoy skiing along the Mississippi River at Coon Rapids Dam or through the pine plantations and sand dunes at Bunker Hills. Chomonix is a golf course squeezed into the vast wetlands of Rice Creek Regional Park. Wargo Nature Center (429-8007) has nature programs and snowshoe rental. FLASH! A four-kilometer ski trail opens in 1997 at Lake George.

BUNKER HILLS REGIONAL PARK

Trackset 18 km (11.1 mi)   **Skate Ski** 5 km (3 mi)

Size 1,599 acres   **Sledding Hill** Unofficial

Rating Easier, except at Archery Range

Warming House Golf Course Clubhouse is open 8 a.m. to 7 p.m. daily and has a restaurant, **no-wax ski rental**, snacks, washrooms and water.

Winter Walking 5.5 miles of paved paths

Bunker Hills, like much of Anoka County, rests on the Anoka Sandplain. Layers of sand and gravel were transported and laid down by melting waters during the retreat of the last glacier. Wind action formed sand dunes and these can best be seen in the archery range (not used in winter) and family camping area just to the north. Pine plantations have helped stabilize the shifting sands. Bunker Hills Park was named after Kendall Bunker who homesteaded here in the 1850s.

The gentle topography of the sandplain makes this an excellent area for beginners. The prettiest trails are through the pine and spruce on the north edge of the golf course. Intermediate and better skiers may choose to try out the steep pitches at the archery range. One chute in particular has left an indelible mark on my mind and my behind.

CHOMONIX SKI TRAILS

Trackset 8.3 km (5.2 mi)   **Skate Ski** 2.4 km (1.5 mi)

Rating Easier   **Size** 2,500 acres

Warming House Open 8 a.m. to 4 p.m. Wednesday through Sunday with snacks, washrooms and **no-wax ski rental**.

The ski trails at Chomonix may be on a golf course but the fact that they are surrounded by vast tracts of wetlands and not expensive tract housing certainly adds to their appeal. Watch for the annual winter festival here with ski lessons and snowshoe walks. Full moon skiing is also scheduled.

COON RAPIDS DAM REGIONAL PARK

East Side administered by Anoka Parks. Phone 757-3920

Trackset 11 km (6.8 mi)   **Skate Ski** Same

Rating Easier   **Size** 600 acres

Warming House Visitor Center open Tuesday through Sunday 8 a.m. to 5 p.m., with vending machines, washrooms and **no-wax ski rental**.

Winter Walking 4.8 km (3 miles) paved and plowed

The mighty Mississippi is the big attraction here and is visible from a number of locations. The skiing isn't particularly exciting but makes for a good family outing.

The trails upstream of the Visitors Center pass through some deep woods, while south of the center the terrain is even more flat and open. In late spring watch for a variety of waterfowl and raptors on the open water below the dam. I have spotted cormorants and buffleheads, and bald eagles are not uncommon.

West Side administered by Hennepin Parks, 424-8172

Hours Open sunrise to sunset **Fee** County pass required

Winter Walking 3 miles, packed snow   **Size** 360 acres

Visitor Center Weekends noon to 5 p.m. Call for weekday hours. Nature programs, natural history exhibits with live animals, sodas, water and washrooms.

Snowshoeing Guided hikes and **snowshoe rental.**

The mighty Mississippi is the main attraction for visitors. The walkway on the Coon Rapids Dam will be completed by the summer of 1997 and provides a spectacular viewing platform. Watch for migrating birds early and late in winter, waterfowl and eagles anytime on the open water.

LAKE GEORGE REGIONAL PARK

Park entrance is at 217th Av. N.W. just east of Lake George Blvd. (Co. Rd. 9). About four kilometers of trails will be tracked for easy skiing. Portapotty only.

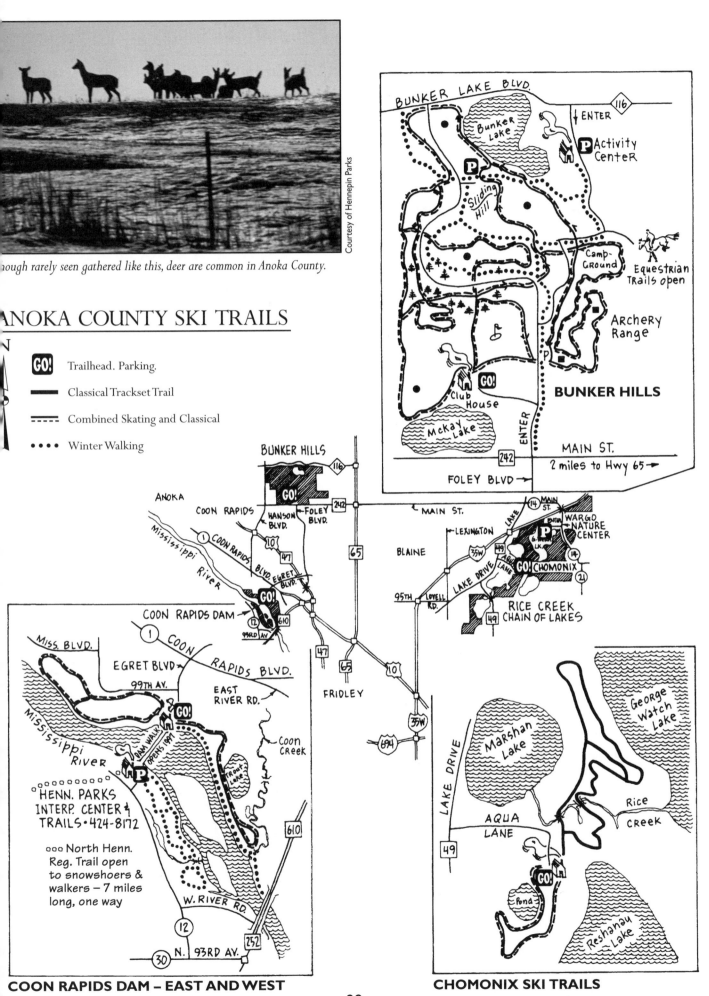

Although rarely seen gathered like this, deer are common in Anoka County.

Courtesy of Hennepin Parks

ANOKA COUNTY SKI TRAILS

GO! Trailhead. Parking.

—— Classical Trackset Trail

--- Combined Skating and Classical

•••• Winter Walking

BUNKER HILLS

BUNKER LAKE BLVD.

ENTER 116

Bunker Lake

P Activity Center

P

Sliding Hill

Camp-Ground

Equestrian Trails open

Archery Range

Club House

GO!

McKay Lake

ENTER

MAIN ST.

242 FOLEY BLVD → 2 miles to Hwy 65 →

ANOKA

COON RAPIDS

BUNKER HILLS 116

GO!

242

HANSON BLVD. FOLEY BLVD.

MAIN ST.

10 47

65

BLAINE

LEXINGTON

35W

95TH LOVELL RD.

14 MAIN ST.

P WARGO NATURE CENTER

49

GO! CHOMONIX 14 21

RICE CREEK CHAIN OF LAKES

Mississippi River 1 COON RAPIDS BLVD. EGRET BLVD.

COON RAPIDS DAM →

12 610 93RD AV.

47

65

10

694

FRIDLEY

35W

COON RAPIDS DAM – EAST AND WEST

MISS. BLVD.

Mississippi River

EGRET BLVD. → 99TH AV.

COON RAPIDS BLVD.

EAST RIVER RD. →

Coon Creek

GO!

DAM WALK OPENS 1991

P

Trout Lake

HENN. PARKS INTERP. CENTER & TRAILS • 424-8172

ooo North Henn. Reg. Trail open to snowshoers & walkers – 7 miles long, one way

W. RIVER RD.

12

30 N. 93RD AV. 252 610

CHOMONIX SKI TRAILS

George Watch Lake

Marshan Lake

Rice Creek

LAKE DRIVE

AQUA LANE

49

GO!

Pond

Reshanau Lake

- 29 -

3 ARCOLA TRAIL

Administered by National Park Service   Phone 430-1938 or 715-635-8346

GO! Take Hwy 95 out of Stillwater and two miles north of Hwy. 96 take a right on Arcola Trail Road. Proceed two miles to Rivard Road (first road south of railroad tracks). Unmarked trail starts just north of Rivard.

Trail 6 km (3.8 mi) not tracked or groomed   **Hours** Daily, 24 hours   **Size** 207 acres

Rating Mostly level but rated intermediate due to steep trail connections and unmaintained trails.

Fee Free   **Amenities** None

Snowshoeing and Winter Walking Allowed. Please stay off ski tracks.

*A*dventurous skiers and snowshoers will discover a gorgeous riverside setting framed by the spectacular Soo Line High Bridge.

If you enjoy a bit of bushwacking and don't mind not knowing exactly where you are, the Arcola trails ramble through a beautiful parcel of the St. Croix River Valley. While not heavily used, this area is open to hunting as well as hiking and skiing.

It's worth venturing out on these trails just to get a good look at the 1911 Soo Line High Bridge as it dances half a mile across the river at a height of 184 feet. In his book *Bridges: Spans of North America,* David Plowder calls the High Bridge "one of the most sublime examples of a steel bridge, and the only American design that can be compared with the magnificent iron creations of Eiffel's in France and Portugal."

Along the trails you will also find a beautiful stone wall that was part of the former summer estate of St. Paul's Heath family, old growth pine and cedar, plus a beautiful little creek trail that leads to a four-star view of the bridge.

Private property, including the bridge, surrounds this area, so don't wander too far. An obvious north-south trail follows an 1884 Wisconsin Central Railway bed while two old roads lead down to the river.

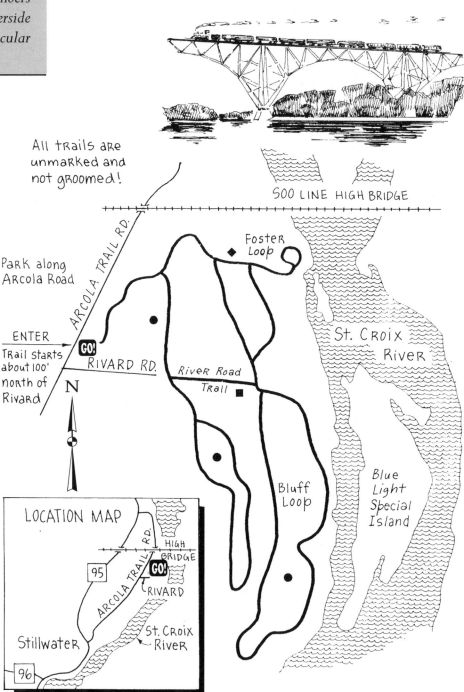

All trails are unmarked and not groomed!

SOO LINE HIGH BRIDGE

ARCOLA TRAIL RD.

Park along Arcola Road

Foster Loop

ENTER
Trail starts about 100' north of Rivard

GO! RIVARD RD.

N

River Road Trail

St. Croix River

Bluff Loop

Blue Light Special Island

LOCATION MAP

HIGH BRIDGE

95

ARCOLA TRAIL RD.

GO! RIVARD

Stillwater

St. Croix River

96

BAKER PARK RESERVE

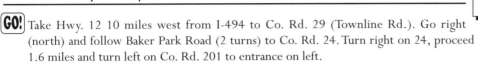

Administered by Hennepin Parks   Phone 473-4114   Trails Hotline 559-6778

GO! Take Hwy. 12 10 miles west from I-494 to Co. Rd. 29 (Townline Rd.). Go right (north) and follow Baker Park Road (2 turns) to Co. Rd. 24. Turn right on 24, proceed 1.6 miles and turn left on Co. Rd. 201 to entrance on left.

Trackset 11.5 km (7.1 mi)   **Skate Ski** 9.5 km (5.9 mi)   **Size** 2,700 acres

Rating Meticulously groomed trails for intermediate level skiers

Fee Park permit ($4/day, $25/year), MN Ski Pass   **Hours** Sunrise to sunset

Warming House 10 to 5 weekdays, 9 to 5 weekends. Good variety of concessions, washrooms, and both **skate ski** and **no-wax ski rental**.

Snowshoeing A 100-acre area has been set aside for snowshoe exploration. **Snowshoe rental** available.

Sliding Hill near warming house. **Camping** site on Half Moon Lake has a shelter with wood stove and table.

First in the line of great Hennepin Parks. Baker caters to winter sports enthusiasts — skiers, sliders and snowshoers of all ages. Best groomed trails in town — ask Greg LeMond.

On January 4, 1956, Morris T. Baker announced a gift of 210 acres on Lake Independence for use as a park. Four months later Maple Hill County Park opened and Hennepin Parks system was under way.

Many skiers in the Twin Cities have been discouraged by the fickle weather and snow conditions of the mid-1990s. Thaws followed by deep freezes, sleet and rain made the snow outside their houses a mess for walking let alone skiing. Yet through most of these winters Baker has offered ski conditions that were good to excellent.

Using two state-of-the-art grooming machines, Hennepin Parks can take the lightest snows — or the crustiest ice — and lay a track you won't believe. And they do it daily.

The Scandinavian-modern ski chalet (aka golf clubhouse) is the center of activities for this bustling area. The rolling terrain is plenty of fun, while lakes, hardwoods and marsh paint a scenic backdrop.

Lessons and rental equipment are available for both skate skiing and traditional cross country. With a little practice you may even want to try your luck in the annual **Baker Shaker Ski Race** that takes place the end of January for kids from 6 to 96.

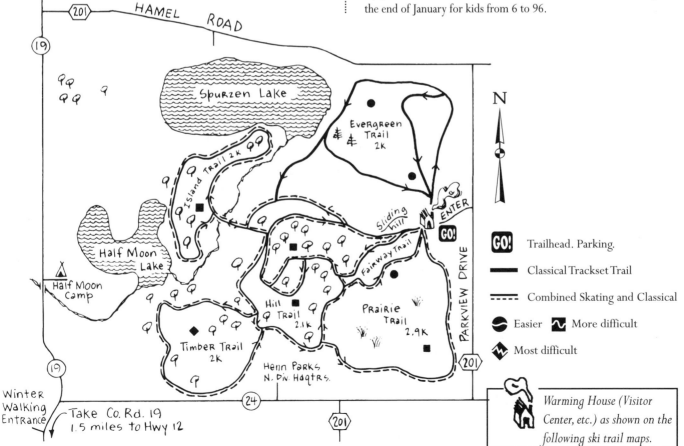

5 BANNING STATE PARK

Administered by Minnesota DNR   Phone 320-245-2668

GO! Located about 75 miles north of the Twin Cities. Exit I-35 at Highway 23 (12 miles north of Hinckley) and go right (east) 1/4 mile to park entrance on right.

Trackset 19.3 km (12 mi)   **Skate Ski** None   **Size** 6,500 acres

Rating Groomed, mostly easier   **Hours** 8 a.m. to 10 p.m.   **Fee** $4 two-day, $20 annual pass

Warming House Heated office has indoor toilet, water, limited space. Office usually open 8 to 4:30 p.m. weekends and 10 to 2 p.m. weekdays. Outdoor toilet otherwise.

The famed Kettle River rapids are magical when sheathed with ice. The handsome and historic Quarry Trail is equally attractive. This is a great day trip.

Banning State Park has all the ingredients for a great day trip — plenty of trails for all levels of skiers, a couple of great picnic spots, some intriguing history and the singular beauty of Banning Rapids. It is a place that invites exploration — to Wolf Creek Falls or the Bat Cave (ask for directions). And a place that tickles the imagination with huge stone slabs from the abandoned quarry, remnant white pine from a once vast forest, and roaring rapids awaiting their springtime frolic with kayaks and covered canoes.

William L. Banning was president of the St. Paul and Duluth Railroad when the line that passes through the park was completed between the two cities. The town of Banning grew to a population of 300 at the turn of the century before the use of structural steel closed all quarry operations.

Today, you can enjoy a self-guided trail through the old quarry and townsite for both its historic and scenic qualities. The dark pink *Hinkley Sandstone* that was quarried here can be seen at Minneapolis City Hall and at Pillsbury Hall on the University of Minnesota campus.

This is a beautiful place to ski, and I have fond memories of gliding through groves of paper birch trees. Take off your skis and walk down to the secluded pine and birch-filled glen that shelters Wolf Creek Falls. Or stop up on the first Sunday in February to participate in the annual **American Cancer Society Skiathon.** A candlelight ski takes place the second weekend in February, and lucky skiers have even heard the sound of wolves howling.

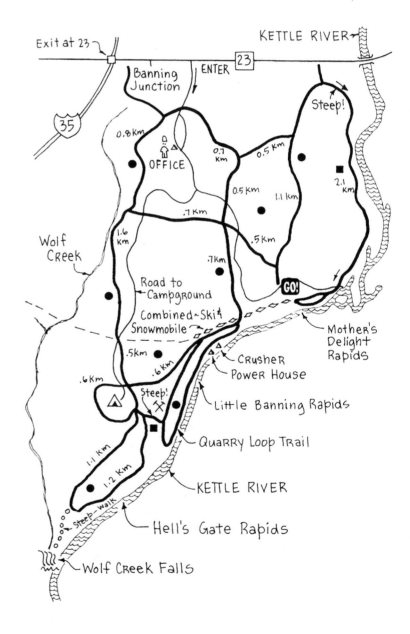

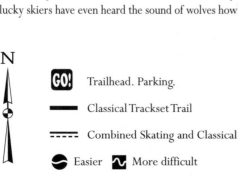

N

GO!   Trailhead. Parking.

————   Classical Trackset Trail

- - - -   Combined Skating and Classical

● Easier   〰 More difficult

6 BATTLE CREEK REGIONAL PARK

Administered by Ramsey County   Phone 777-1707

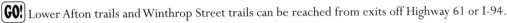

GO! Lower Afton trails and Winthrop Street trails can be reached from exits off Highway 61 or I-94.

Trackset Lower Afton 8 km (5 mi); Winthrop 6 km (3.7 mi)   **Skate Ski** Winthrop only, same length

Fee None, MN Ski Pass required   **Size** 800 acres (2,200 total)   **Hours** Sunrise to sunset

Rating Both sites are well-groomed with challenging hills. Winthrop site is most difficult. Lower Afton has one easier loop.

Warming House Generally not available, outdoor toilet only

Sliding Hill Winthrop Street site   **Winter Walking** 1.5 mile loop at Upper Afton. Two-mile ravine path opens in 1998.

*B*oth sites have great trails for better skiers and are within easy reach. Surprise! They are *wonderfully underutilized.*

Someday Battle Creek Park may sport the finest urban ski system in the country. The park sprawls over several hundred acres and contains a beautiful ravine, lively creek and steep blufftop terrain covered by a mature hardwood forest. The master plan calls for a 20-kilometer trail system to link all the park segments together.

While this plan will take several years to unfold, over two kilometers of trails were added to the Winthrop site in 1995, and lighting may soon follow.

Both areas are well worth a visit even if you must travel across the river. The Winthrop site commands high ground with views over the Mississippi River Valley. A ski jump and small downhill ski area no longer exist but kids now get their kicks on one of the areas steeper sliding hills.

The Lower Afton site has terrain for all levels of skiers and enjoys a canopy of mature hardwoods, with several ponds sprinkled among the rolling glacial terrain.

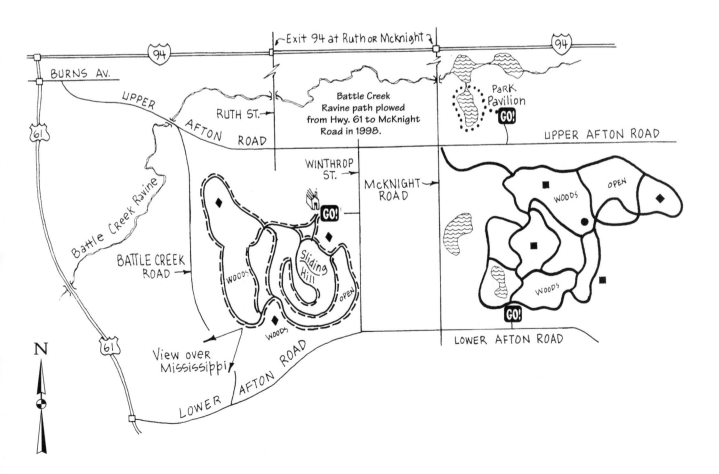

BLOOMINGTON TRAILS

Administered by City of Bloomington   Phone 948-8877

Trails HYLAND LAKE PARK RESERVE (see page 52) is the only park that has groomed trails. TIERNEY'S WOODS (intermediate), NINE MILE CREEK (easier along the creek), and the MINNESOTA RIVER TRAIL (easier) are open sunrise to 10 p.m. (or as posted) for skiing or snowshoeing on an informal basis. Outdoor toilets at Normandale only.

Winter Walking NORMANDALE LAKE TRAILS (paved and plowed) and GIRARD LAKE PARK (woodchip, not plowed) are enjoyed for winter walking.

Skating and Sledding Running Park and Westwood (skate only). Warming house at both places.

TIERNEY'S WOODS

Trail 2.4 km (1.5 mi) hilly   **Size** 138 acres

This is a beautiful remnant of the Big Woods that once reached from here to St. Cloud. Some trees are well over 200 years old. This place is rarely visited and the narrow paths wander around, sometimes disappearing into squirrel trails.

MT. NORMANDALE LAKE PARK

Trail 3.2 km (2 mi) level   **Size** 185 acres

The paved walking and running path that circles the shallow 135-acre lake is plowed in winter and extremely popular.

GIRARD LAKE PARK

Trail 1.7 km (1 mi) level   **Size** 61 acres

A small, pretty park with a woodchip path around the namesake lake. Skiing is allowed but most folks walk.

GO! Trailhead. Parking.

⎯⎯ Ski Trail — (some OK to walk)

•••• Winter Walking

MINNESOTA RIVER TRAIL

Trail 16 km (10 mi) one way with some hills east of Lyndale.

New trailheads at the end of Lyndale Avenue and next to the old Bloomington Ferry Bridge will make access to this unique area easier than ever. This is a great place to explore on foot, snowshoes or skis. Come prepared as there are no facilities and you will be travelling through isolated and unmarked terrain. Wildlife is plentiful, and stretches of this trail have been trod for centuries.

NINE MILE CREEK

Trail 8 km (5 mi) mostly flat   **Size** 522 acres

Trailheads are located behind City Hall on Old Shakopee Road, at Moir Park on Morgan Av., and where 106th St. crosses the ravine. Nine Mile Creek flows through a deep wooded ravine. The trail follows the bubbling stream on its scenic journey to the Minnesota River. Skiers should visit promptly after a new snowfall as winter walkers predominate. The creek's name refers to its distance from Fort Snelling.

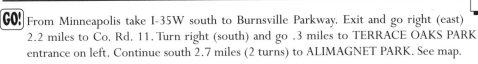

GO! From Minneapolis take I-35W south to Burnsville Parkway. Exit and go right (east) 2.2 miles to Co. Rd. 11. Turn right (south) and go .3 miles to TERRACE OAKS PARK entrance on left. Continue south 2.7 miles (2 turns) to ALIMAGNET PARK. See map.

Fee MN Ski Pass pending   **Hours** Sunrise to 10 p.m.

TERRACE OAKS PARK

Trackset 11 km (6.8 mi)   **Skate Ski** Same length

Size 230 acres

Rating Some of the best hills in the metro area. Well groomed.

Warming House Open 1:30 to 5:30 p.m. Mon. to Fri., 10:30 to 5:30 p.m. on weekends. Concessions, washrooms and **ski rental**.

A great place for good skiers to test their wings. The beautiful oak woods are a joy for all.

Terrace Oaks has a rollicking terrain of hummocks, hills and depressions. Low lying marshes and ponds balance the red and white oak-covered hills. The lone open hillside just north of the warming house is a rare remnant oak savanna — grassland with solitary burr oaks rising above.

Ski lessons are available (call for times) and local high schools use the well-designed trails for training. This is a great city park preserve with regional appeal. And to think it nearly ended up a golf course.

ALIMAGNET PARK

Trackset 4.7 km (2.9 mi)   **Skate Ski** Same length

Size 178 acres

Rating Easier to intermediate with a few decent hills in the woods.

Warming House No   **Toilet** Outdoors

A quiet setting overlooking Alimagnet Lake.

A good getaway if you live nearby and you're not up for the faster moving traffic at Terrace Oaks. The large open ballfields that greet you are a bit of a turn-off, but the wooded perimeter rising above the lake is pleasant and the back half of the trail system is heavily wooded.

Apple Valley has a 100-acre park on the east side of Alimagnet that provides a nice buffer from nearby housing as well as some ungroomed trails you may wish to explore.

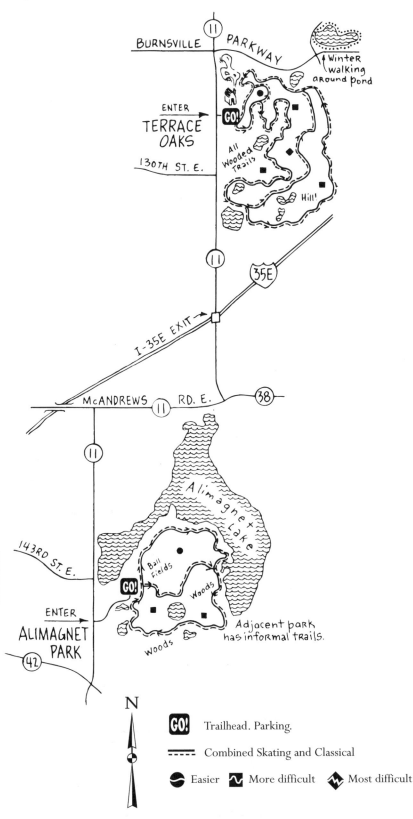

GO! Trailhead. Parking.

- - - - Combined Skating and Classical

● Easier   〰 More difficult   ◆ Most difficult

CANNON VALLEY TRAIL

Administered by Joint Powers Board   Phone 507-263-3954 or (612) 258-4141

GO! Trailheads are located in the picturesque towns of Cannon Falls, Red Wing and Welch. See map below and signs as you enter each town.

Trackset 31.5 km (19.7 mi)   **Skate Ski** Same length

Rating Flat, rail-trail that is tracked, not groomed. The untracked Cannon Valley Interpretive Trail is rated more difficult.

Fee MN Ski Pass required   **Hours** Sunrise to 10 p.m.

Amenities Portapotty at Welch Station Acess. Welch Village Ski Area is full service. **Untracked Loops** 3.2 km (2 mi)

Easy skiing through a deep, secluded valley crowned with handsome rock outcroppings. Wild turkeys and bald eagles may be your only companions.

Nestled along the base of a north-facing bluff, the Cannon Valley Trail holds its snow long after many Twin Cities ski trails have turned brown. Most folks have experienced the charms of this beautiful trail from the seat of a bicycle. In winter, the green curtain drops and the rock cliffs and rushing stream are more easily seen. It is also readily apparent that the flocks of people have disappeared. In their place you may get lucky and see some wild turkeys gathered together. Trail manager Bruce Blair counted 45 in one flock recently. Bruce also spots bald eagles almost daily coming up from the Mississippi and notes that some robins spend the winter at open creeks.

Welch is the most common access point. Some families may choose to split up into downhill and cross country ski contingents. Welch Village has all the comforts of home plus the lively jostling of the downhill crowd.

Two untracked ski loops are located between Cannon Falls and Welch. At the Anderson Memorial Rest Area, a half-mile loop takes you through a dense floodplain forest. Skiers craving a little excitement can take the 1.5 mile Cannon Valley Interpretive Trail loop that climbs to a terrace 100 feet above the valley floor. Signs point out forest management techniques but you'll probably be more interested in paying attention to the speedy downhill runs.

The Cannon Valley is renowned for its unique geology, native plants, wildlife and human activity that date back nearly 10,000 years. Bruce Blair's *Guide to the Lower Cannon River Valley* is an excellent resource for further exploration.

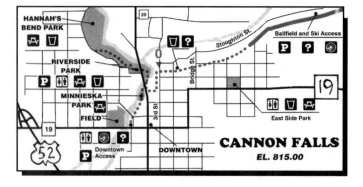

CANNON FALLS EL. 815.00

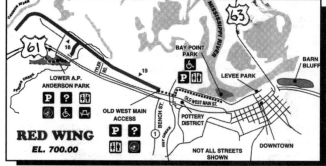

RED WING EL. 700.00

Administered by Carver County   Phone 467-4200

Fee $3 daily, MN Ski Pass required   **Hours** Sunrise to sunset

BAYLOR REGIONAL PARK

GO! Take State Hwy. 212 28 miles south and west of I-494 to Young America. Take Co. Rd. 33 right (north) 2.4 miles to park entrance on right.

Trackset 8 km (5 mi)   **Size** 201 acres

Rating Beginner trails groomed weekly.

Warming House Open 8 a.m. to sunset daily. Washrooms, water, candy and **no-wax ski rental**.

A natural oasis for skiing, sledding and sky gazing amidst the farmland.

Baylor Regional Park is located in the extreme southwest corner of Metroland, so far removed from the city that it was the perfect place to watch Comet Hyakutake as it swept past Earth in late March 1995.

Perched on the shoulder of Eagle Lake and surrounded by farmers' fields, Baylor preserves a rich mix of native habitat. A large grove of mature maple trees are tapped in early spring each year for maple syrup. Trails also pass through marsh, meadow and along Eagle Lake.

LAKE MINNEWASHTA REGIONAL PARK

GO! Take Hwy. 7 seven miles west from I-494 to Hwy. 41. Turn left (south) and proceed one mile to entrance on right.

Trackset 8.5 km (5.3 mi)   **Size** 350 acres

Rating Beginner and intermediate trails groomed weekly.

Amenities Outdoor toilet

Big oaks, some hills and a lakeside jaunt are yours alone for the taking.

An overlooked park with a remnant of the Big Woods that once covered this area. There is some nice skiing here, especially in the rolling woods north of the entrance. You probably have a better chance of seeing deer than people while visiting.

A couple of the oaks are over 12 feet in circumference — big enough to be registered with the DNR. An ambitious reforestation project planting 25,000 hardwoods is complete but will take several years to recreate the leafy canopy that once covered the park.

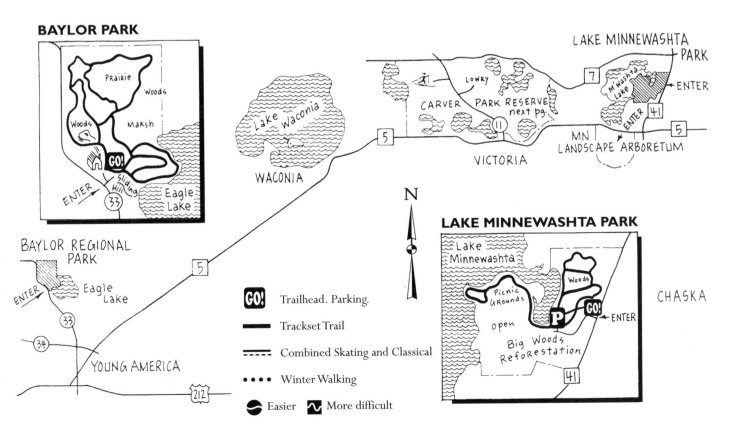

CARVER PARK RESERVE

Administered by Hennepin Parks, 559-9000 or 446-1801, Trails Hotline 559-6778

GO! Take Hwy. 5 twelve miles west from I-494 to Co. Rd. 11. Turn right (north) on 11 (at the Dairy Queen!) and proceed 2 miles to LOWRY NATURE CENTER entrance on right. The entrance to the ski trailhead is up another mile on left.

Trackset 21 km (13.2 mi)   **Skate Ski** 6.1 km (3.8 mi)   **Size** 3,500 acres

Rating Well groomed trails for beginner and intermediate level skiing

Fee Park permit ($4/day, $25/year), Mn Ski Pass required   **Hours** Sunrise to sunset

Warming House Wood-heated barn open weekends. Some snacks, outside toilet and **no-wax ski rental**.

LOWRY NATURE CENTER (472-4911) Open 9 a.m. to 5 p.m. Tuesday through Saturday and noon to 5 on Sunday

Snowshoeing Special programs, animal tracking and **snowshoe rental** available.

Sledding Popular hill at Nature Center plus **Norwegian kick-sled rental** for use on hiking trails and at Crosby Lake.

Winter Walking Allowed on Lowry's 6 miles of hiking trails. No dogs!

*N*ear wilderness, near the city. The second largest Hennepin Parks' park reserve and home to the Lowry Nature Center. Kids get their kicks on the sledding hill.

While visiting a Hennepin Parks facility located in Carver County may seem natural today, it was quite controversial when first proposed. Carver Park was authorized for purchase on December 3, 1964. A lawsuit requesting the purchase be found illegal was rejected in April, 1966, and Hennepin Parks went on to purchase park land in Anoka, Scott and Wright counties.

Today, folks throughout the metro area are the beneficiaries of Hennepin Parks' early imperialist urges. Carver Park Reserve has 3,500 acres with lakeshore frontage on six major lakes. These lakes and rolling terrain are typical of the glacial morraine country of west central Minnesota. The land was used for dairy farming until the early 1960s and includes meadow, prairie, wetland and forest.

A large barn serves as the trailhead for cross country skiing at Carver. Many of the trails traverse open hillsides and meadow that are much more pleasant on calm sunny days. The central Lake Trail is the most protected on windswept days.

Lowry Nature Center has a terrific mix of winter programs for kids and adults. Tracking mink, voles and fox, building snowcaves (quinzes!) and bird banding are among the most popular.

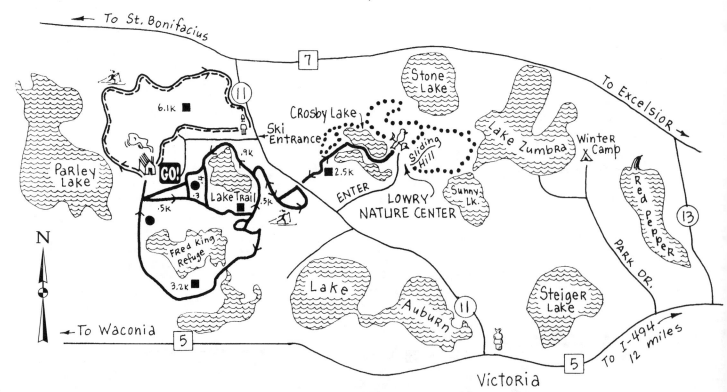

CLEARY LAKE REGIONAL PARK

Administered by Hennepin Parks, phone 447-2171, Trails Hotline 559-6778

GO! Take I-35W or I-35E south and exit at Co. Rd. 42. Go right (west) about 4 miles to Co. Rd. 27. Turn left (south) and go 4 miles to entrance on right.

Trackset 13.3 km (8.3 mi)   **Skate Ski** None   **Size** 1,200 acres

Rating Well groomed and mostly easier. One large hill can be bypassed.

Fee Park permit ($4/day, $25/year), MN Ski Pass required   **Hours** Sunrise to sunset

Warming House Open weekends and some weekdays. Call first. Fireplace, concessions including hot chocolate, washrooms and **no-wax ski rental.**

Camping Walk-in primitive campsite plus group camp.

Good traditional skiing for beginners and families. Lessons are available on the relatively flat, non-threatening trails.

This Hennepin Parks' facility is slightly off the beaten path — as a matter of fact, it's in Scott County. This is the only Hennepin Parks trail where skate skiing is not allowed, adding to the relaxed ambiance out on the trail.

When I first visited over ten years ago I noted that "relative remoteness means it has fewer visitors." Today the encroaching housing developments make Cleary Lake feel more like a natural oasis than a seamless part of the farmland and countryside. Hennepin Parks must be commended for their farsightedness in preserving this area. The landscape consists of gentle hills of old pasture, sizable hardwood forest and swampy lowlands. Deer and a good variety of woodpeckers are winter residents.

Warming House (Visitor Center, etc.) as shown on the ski trail maps.

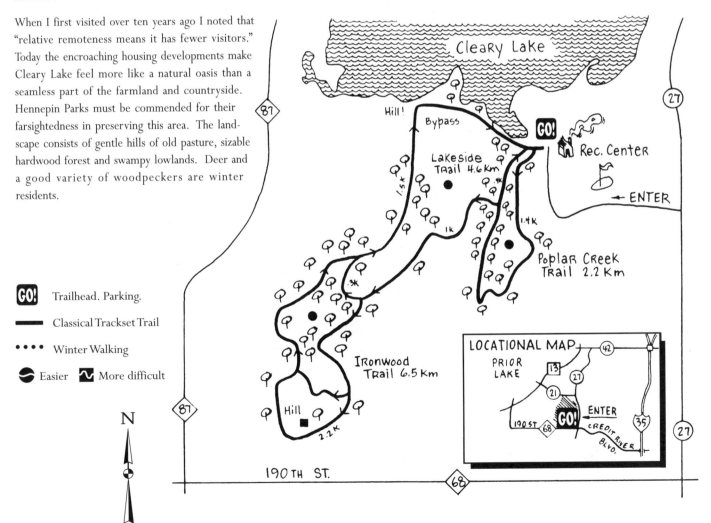

GO! Trailhead. Parking.

——— Classical Trackset Trail

• • • • Winter Walking

Easier   More difficult

N

COMO REGIONAL PARK

Administered by City of St. Paul   Phone 266-6400   Ski Center Phone 488-9673

Trackset 7 km (4.3 mi)   **Skate Ski** Same length

Rating Beginner to intermediate with a 3 km lighted trail. Groomed three times a week.

Fee Free, MN Ski Pass required   **Hours** 6 a.m. to 11 p.m.   **Size** 450 acres

Warming House Beautiful, glass-walled clubhouse is open weekdays 3 to 9 p.m., Sat. 9 to 6 p.m., Sun 11 a.m. to
6 p.m. and has good food (burgers, fries, etc.), washrooms and **no-wax ski rental**.

Downhill Skiing Small area has 2 rope tows, rental equipment, snowmaking and a 70-foot-vertical drop.
Very popular for beginner's lessons and cheap!

Skating The tradition continues at the Lakeside Pavilion. Phone 488-4920 for conditions.

Winter Walking 1.7 mile path around Como Lake, free **Zoo** and the tropical splendor of the **Conservatory**.

St. Paul's most beloved park is Minnesota's oldest and offers something for everyone most evenings and all winter long.

When the snow flies the golf clubhouse becomes a ski chalet and fairly bustling center for both cross country and (surprise!) downhill skiing. There's a small sledding hill for kiddies, and a skating rink is maintained next to the Lakeside Pavilion.

Even with its long tradition as a recreational retreat Como can still surprise. I was resting a moment while cross country skiing one night when I was startled by the howling of a wolf from the Zoo next door. Park officials continue to monitor sporting trends and may groom trails for snowshoeing and dog "ski-jouring" at the "40 acres" parcel shown on the map.

The land for Como was purchased in 1873 for the then outrageous sum of $100,000. In recent years millions of dollars have been spent to rebuild and rejuvenate this perennial favorite.

A great place for a post 9 to 5 workout, Como also caters to beginning skiers looking for lessons to improve their technique. The Lalapalooza Loppett cross country ski race happens the third Sunday in January. And if you can't swing a trip to Hawaii in the middle of winter, a visit to the Conservatory is the next best thing. The soaring palm trees and warm, moist air will either soothe your nerves or have you booking the next flight south.

14 COTTAGE GROVE RAVINE REGIONAL PARK

Administered by Washington County   Phone 731-3851

GO! From St. Paul head south on Highway 61 twelve miles (from I-94) and exit at
Keats Av. — Chemolite Road (Co. Rd. 19). Go left (northwest) 1/8 mile to the
frontage road and right (southeast) 1/2 mile to entrance on left.

Trackset 11.3 km (7 mi)   **Skate Ski** 3 km (1.9 mi)   **Size** 450 acres

Rating Mostly intermediate, with some expert hills in back. Easier loop around pond.

Fee County Pass ($4 day/$16 year), MN Ski Pass   **Hours** 7 a.m. to 1/2 hour after sunset

Warming House Heated with wood fire   **Toilet** Indoors   **Rental** No

*Picturesque ravines with some fast moving trails and a beautiful pine plantation make
Cottage Grove Ravine a personal favorite.*

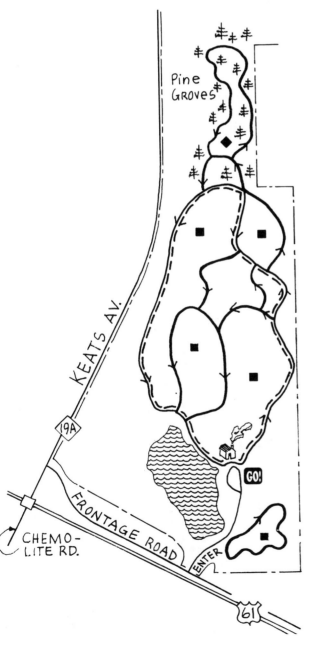

This is a handsome park that stays pretty quiet except for when the
high school teams are practicing. The park name refers to the nearby
town (organized in May 1858), and the wooded ravine that was
formed in glacial times and may once have been a channel of the St.
Croix River.

This is a great park for the experienced skier, with almost 150 feet in
elevation change and some great downhill runs. It is also an excellent place to try some ski skating. The long stretch nearest Keats
Avenue is ramped slightly downhill which helps considerably. And
there are some precipitous drops through the groves of Norway pines
that recall skiing on the North Shore.

Be on the lookout for pileated woodpeckers. These spectacular birds
with a flaming red crest can reach 16 inches in height. If a loud jack-
hammering sound breaks the silence, you'll know they are close by.

N

GO! Trailhead. Parking.

———— Classical Trackset Trail

- - - - Combined Skating and Classical

⊖ Easier   ⚡ More difficult   ⚡ Most difficult

SKI 15 CROW-HASSAN PARK RESERVE

Administered by Hennepin Parks   Phone 559-9000   Trail Hotline 559-6778

GO! Take I-94 9.5 miles north from I-494 to Rogers. Exit and go south (left) 1.2 miles on Co. Rd. 150 (Main St.) to Co. Rd. 116 (Territorial Road). Turn right and go 2.5 miles to Hassan Parkway. Turn left and go 2 miles to park entrance just north of T-intersection.

Trackset 17.6 km (10.9 mi)   **Skate Ski** 10.1 km (6.3 mi)   **Size** 2,600 acres

Rating Intermediate to expert level skiing on longer trail system

Fee Park permit ($4/day, $25/year) MN Ski Pass required   **Hours** Sunrise to sunset

Warming House Weekends only 9 a.m. to 5 p.m., snacks   **Toilet** Outdoors

Winter Camping Ski-in camping at the Blue Stem Campsite with shelter, wood stove and table.

> *A favorite destination for those in the know. Long, challenging trails through prairie and woodland. Excellent grooming. Solitude.*

It's hard to imagine an endless sea of grass flowing from Minnesota to the Rocky Mountains now that trees, crops, houses and billboards muddy the view. But one of the best places in the Twin Cities to catch a glimpse of that sweeping landscape is Crow-Hassan Park Reserve where 600 acres of old farm field have been transformed back into prairie.

The reintroduction of native grasses and forbes began here in 1969 using seeds from a two-acre remnant of virgin prairie located in the park near Prairie Lake. Other sources were also tapped to complete the collection of nearly 100 species that have been planted.

Skate skiing through a glowing field of undulating grasses in the morning sun is a thrill better experienced than described on paper. Crow-Hassan is listed by many longtime skiers as being their favorite park, and it's easy to see why. Even though they have closed the most hair-raising downhill trail, there are still plenty of drops to get excited about. The trails are well groomed each weekend and, most importantly, the park is big enough and remote enough that crowding is never an issue. Check it out.

N

 **GO!** Trailhead. Parking.

 Classical Trackset Trail

Combined Skating and Classical

 Easier   More difficult   Most difficult

EAGAN SKI TRAILS

Administered by City of Eagan   Phone 681-4660

GO! See map below for park locations.   **Fee** Free

Hours Sunrise to sunset. TRAPP FARM PARK SLIDING HILL hours below.

> *Eagan has two fine parks for intermediate level skiing and a free (yes, free!) tubing hill for kids of all ages.*

BLACKHAWK PARK

Trackset 1.6 km (1 mi)   **Size** 82 acres

Rating Intermediate or better

Warming House Water and washrooms in minimally heated shelter.

Sledding Yes. Informal but OK.

Winter Walking About a 1 mile path

This is a fun little area for better skiers. A good downhill run takes you into the park, and the surrounding development is only noticeable along the western perimeter. Some remnant native prairie can be found amid the meadows and marsh. Large oaks, maple and birch surround these open areas. The warming house was just completed in 1996, and additional winter activities are being considered.

PATRICK EAGAN PARK

Trackset 3.2 km (2 mi)   **Size** 102 acres

Rating Intermediate

It's a long way from Tipperary, Ireland, but the town's namesake arrived here in 1853 and staked a claim of 220 acres. Patrick became the first chair of the township's board of supervisors and is remembered here in the city's largest and most natural park.

This is a gem of a city park, centrally located but quite isolated in feeling. The park sits in a large bowl focused on McCarthy Lake. Groves of planted pine trees and birch nicely offset the upland hardwoods. Sure, there are plenty of deer here but the pair of coyotes found hanging around in 1996 raised even more eyebrows.

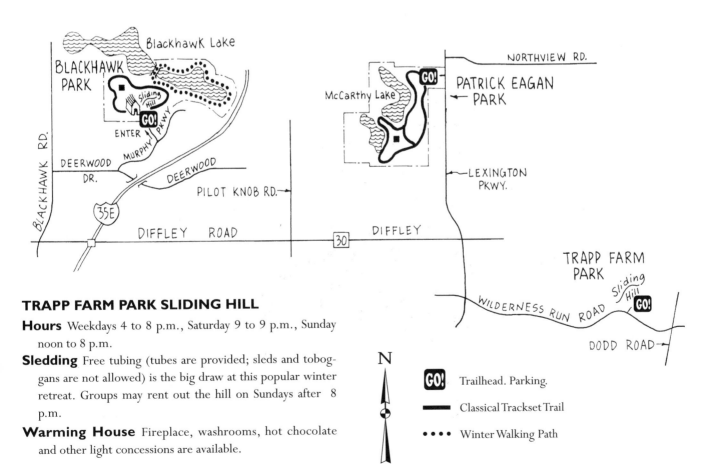

TRAPP FARM PARK SLIDING HILL

Hours Weekdays 4 to 8 p.m., Saturday 9 to 9 p.m., Sunday noon to 8 p.m.

Sledding Free tubing (tubes are provided; sleds and toboggans are not allowed) is the big draw at this popular winter retreat. Groups may rent out the hill on Sundays after 8 p.m.

Warming House Fireplace, washrooms, hot chocolate and other light concessions are available.

GO! Trailhead. Parking.

——— Classical Trackset Trail

•••• Winter Walking Path

ELK RIVER SKI TRAIL

Administered by City of Elk River   Phone 441-7420

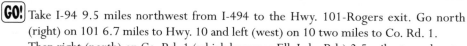

GO! Take I-94 9.5 miles northwest from I-494 to the Hwy. 101-Rogers exit. Go north (right) on 101 6.7 miles to Hwy. 10 and left (west) on 10 two miles to Co. Rd. 1. Then right (north) on Co. Rd. 1 (which becomes Elk Lake Rd.) 2.5 miles to park entrance on right.

Trackset 15 km (9.3 mi)   **Skate Ski** 20 km (12.4 mi)   **Size** 455 acres

Rating Groomed weekly, with good terrain for beginners and great hills for pros.   **Hours** Sunrise to sunset

Fee No fees or ski pass currently required   **Amenities** Portapotty, biathlon course

This is one of the metro area's finest ski areas. Unheralded and with few amenities, it is still a gem for better skiers.

Great work by Dave Anderson and his colleagues has produced an exceptional course for skate skiing, race training and plain old "let's-get-out-in-the-woods-and-bomb-a-few-hills" skiing. Beginners can enjoy the more level trails that wind around the golf course and along the old Burlington Northern railway.

While work is still in progress there is plenty to enjoy right now. A three-kilometer extension to the Shiely Loop takes skiers to 1,102 feet above sea level – reportedly the highest point in five counties – and 152 feet above the low marshland also within the park.

Members of the Junior and Senior National Biathlon team train here. And while the idea of an Olympic event that combines cross country skiing with shooting rifles always struck me as rather peculiar, it may be best to keep that thought to yourself if you see an armed skier making the rounds.

A lack of signage may cause some confusion on the trails but the rail-trail spine is an easily recognizable landmark. The wooded terrain attracts an abundance of wildlife. Watch for coyote tracks, grouse and deer as you're travelling through.

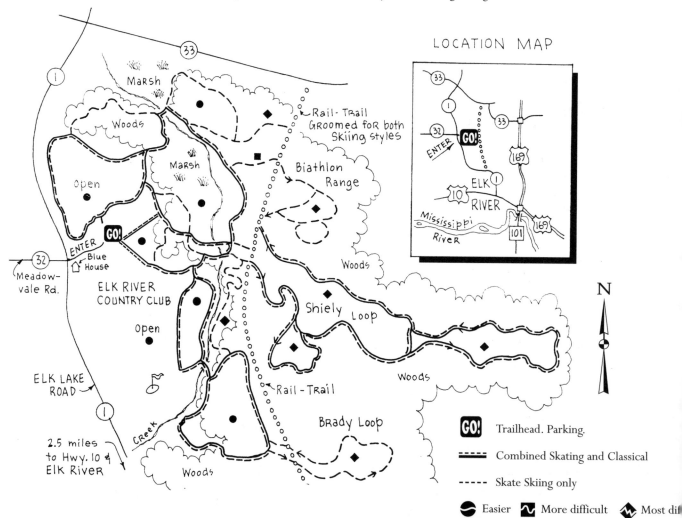

18 ELM CREEK PARK RESERVE

Administered by Hennepin Parks   Phone 424-5511   Trail Hotline 559-6778

GO! Take I-94 3 miles north of I-494 to 93rd Av. N. exit. Go right (east) on 93rd 1 mile to Fernbrook Lane and then left (north) 1.4 miles to Territorial Rd. Turn right (east) and go 1 mile to entrance on left.

Trackset 14.7 km (9.2 mi)   **Skate Ski** 11.5 km (7.1 mi)   **Size** 4,900 acres

Rating Easy to intermediate skiing with no death-defying downhills

Fee Park permit ($4/day, $25/year), MN Ski Pass required   **Hours** Sunrise to sunset

Warming House 10 to 5 weekdays, 9 to 5 weekends. Hot and cold snacks and drinks, washrooms and **ski rental**.

Snowshoeing Rental at EASTMAN NATURE CENTER (phone 420-4300) which has a 4-mile packed snow trail.

Sliding Hill Groomed (!) sliding hill behind warming house   **Winter Walking** Walk on park road closed to traffic.

> *H*ennepin Parks largest park reserve is home to the Eastman Nature Center. A popular spot for sledding, skiing and snowshoeing. A lit five-kilometer ski trail opens in 1998.

Coyotes are now known to roam the wilds of Elm Creek Park Reserve. And while your chances of seeing one are slim their presence attests to the wide expanse of undeveloped land contained here. Five lakes, three streams and 4,900 acres of wetlands, hardwood forest and reclaimed farmland provide plenty of elbow room for wildlife and park-goers alike.

Eastman Nature Center (separate entrance off Elm Creek Road) is the place to go for nature programs, interpretive hikes and the ever-popular deer watches. On late afternoon weekend days in January and February, Eastman packs them in to view the white-tailed deer that come here to feed.

This area has a long history of human activity starting with the Indian tribes that found good hunting grounds here 200 years and more ago. In the 1850s a colony of Swiss settled near Hayden Lake (just north and east of the nature center). They bred cattle, made cheese, raised crops and — like the Native Americans before them — produced maple syrup from nearby sugar bush. Tapping maple syrup still marks the transition from winter to spring.

N

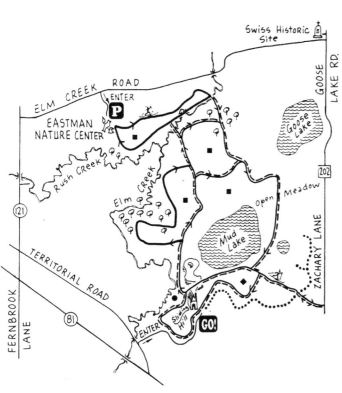

GO! Trailhead. Parking.

—— Classical Trackset Trail

---- Combined Skating and Classical

◖ Easier   ∿ More difficult   ◆ Most difficult

•••• Winter Walking

∘∘∘∘ **North Hennepin Regional Trail**

This seven-mile-long trail runs parallel to, and just north of, 101st Av. N. between Elm Creek Park Reserve and Coon Rapids Dam (see page 29). It is mostly flat and available for walking and snowshoeing.

SKI
19 FORT SNELLING STATE PARK

Administered by MN DNR   Phone 725-2389 or the Interpretive Center at 726-9247

GO! Main entrance is the Post Road exit off of Hwy. 5, .8 miles northeast of I-494. The "packed" trails on the east side of the Minnesota River can be accessed from Sibley House in Mendota Heights. Take D Street off Hwy. 13.

Trackset 16.6 km (10.3 mi)   **Packed** 12.6 km (7.8 mi)   **Size** 3,300 acres

Rating All trails are easy, groomed weekly.   **Hours** 8 a.m. to 10 p.m.   **Fee** $4 two-day, $20 annual pass

Warming House Office (open daily) and Pike Island Interpretive Center (open weekends) have washrooms and water. Picnic Island has shelter with fireplace and wood.

Snowshoeing Rental at office. OK anywhere except on ski trails.

Winter Walking Packed 3-mile trail on Pike Island or 7.8-mile trail across river.

Big Rivers Trail 4.5 miles packed snow

Easy skiing through an urban wilderness that embraces both the center of the Dakota world and the seat of white settlement.

Perhaps it's ironic that the most accessible untamed land in the Twin Cities lies directly below a fort whose mission was to establish a "civilized" foothold in a "wild" frontier. Fort Snelling was strategically built on the high bluffs overlooking the confluence of two great rivers – the Mississippi and Minnesota. The park has remained natural because most of it lies on the floodplain. The great rivers that carved the park's landscape have also protected it from development.

Fort Snelling State Park's rich history is a long story that will be better told when the new Visitors Center opens in the fall of 1997. But ski to the end of Pike Island where the two rivers meet and you will be at the MDO-TE MI-NI-SO-TA, the place the Dakota regard as the center of their universe. The first French fur traders mispronounced MDO-TE as Mendota, and the town across the river still goes by this name.

Fort Snelling is a popular area for traditional cross country skiing. You could easily bag a view of some deer if you're out in the early morning or late afternoon. A naturalist leads snowshoeing, back country skiing and other programs throughout the winter. Phone 726-9247. A paved trail is being constructed on the east side of the Minnesota River. This may disrupt trail use until it is completed in 1997. These east side trails are typically packed for skate skiing and are rarely used. One evening I was so immersed in solitude that I nearly jumped out of my boots when a pheasant exploded from some trailside brush.

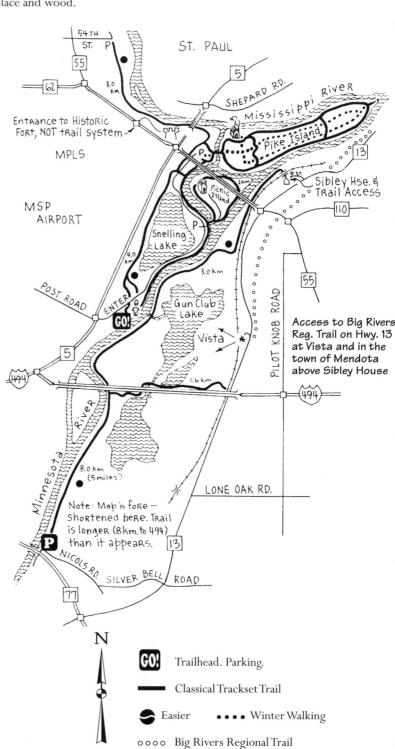

Access to Big Rivers Reg. Trail on Hwy. 13 at Vista and in the town of Mendota above Sibley House

Note: Map is fore-shortened here. Trail is longer (8km. to 494) than it appears.

GO! Trailhead. Parking.

—— Classical Trackset Trail

● Easier   •••• Winter Walking

○○○○ Big Rivers Regional Trail

FRENCH REGIONAL PARK

Administered by Hennepin Parks   Phone 559-8891   Trails Hotline 559-6778

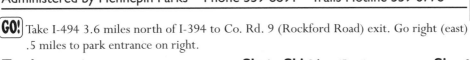

GO! Take I-494 3.6 miles north of I-394 to Co. Rd. 9 (Rockford Road) exit. Go right (east) .5 miles to park entrance on right.

Trackset 9.6 km (6 mi)   **Skate Ski** 8 km (5 mi)   **Size** 310 acres

Rating Mostly intermediate skiing with some steeper pitches on Skyline. The Lagoon Trail is easy.

Fee Park permit ($4/day, $25/year), MN Ski Pass required   **Hours** Sunrise to 9 p.m. daily

Warming House 9 a.m. to 9 p.m. daily with refreshments (fruit to hot dogs), washrooms, **ski rental**

Snowshoeing Naturalist-led trips to beaver lodges   **Sledding Hill** Steep and narrow

Nighttime skiing, city skyline views and a four-star visitor center make this one of Hennepin Parks' most popular destinations.

Clifton E. French was appointed the first superintendent of the Hennepin County Park Reserve District in January 1962. He led the park system through an unprecedented period of development until his retirement in 1984. Under his guidance, Hennepin Parks not only became the largest landowner in the county, it acquired parcels in four adjacent counties.

Originally named Medicine Lake Park, it was renamed and dedicated on August 29, 1985. The park rests atop the large lake known by the Dakota as I (mouth), CA-PA (beaver), CA-GA-STA-KA (free from ice, broken), MDE (lake). While not easily translated, beaver still make their home along the lake and naturalists lead snowshoe hikes to visit their lodges during the winter. (Call for reservations.)

The open landscape of rolling glacial hills is broken along the lake and lagoons with second growth forest. Windy days can be chilly but the fine vista of the downtown Minneapolis skyline in the late afternoon sun is well worth it. This is not a place to come for solitude. The park's central location attracts over 20,000 skiers — half at night — during a good season.

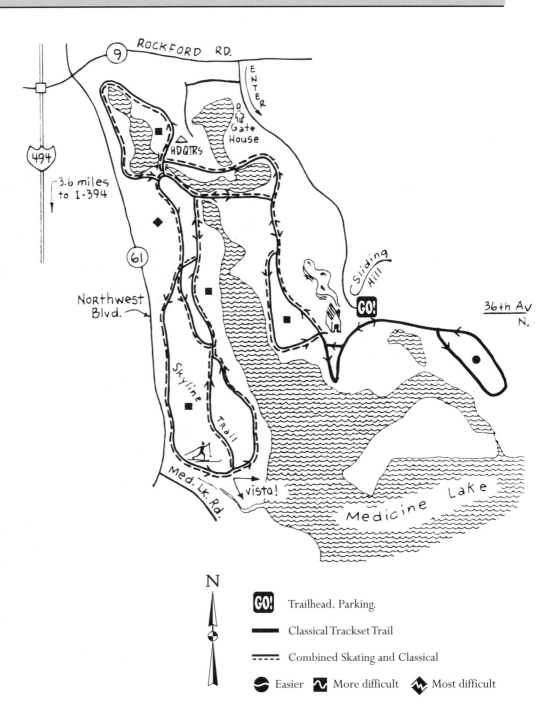

N

GO! Trailhead. Parking.

——— Classical Trackset Trail

- - - - Combined Skating and Classical

Easier   More difficult   Most difficult

FRONTENAC STATE PARK

Administered by Minnesota DNR   Phone 612-345-3401

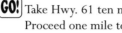

GO! Take Hwy. 61 ten miles south from downtown Red Wing and turn left at Co. Rd. 2. Proceed one mile to entrance on left.

Trackset 12.8 km (8 mi)   **Skate Ski** Same length   **Size** 3,500 acres

Rating Trails are mostly easier but the ravine trail to blufftop is more difficult.

Fee $4 two-day, $20 annual pass   **Hours** 8 a.m. to 10 p.m.

Warming House Wood-heated shelter near entrance. Washroom in office.

Sledding Hill Near office, groomed   **Winter Walking** OK on lightly used, 12-mile snowmobile trail

*B*ig views and big birds (bald eagles) are the chief wintertime attractions.

Frontenac State Park commands high ground with a panoramic blufftop vista that embraces a 20 mile sweep of Lake Pepin — that grand bulge in the Mississippi River formed by the natural damming effect of the Chippewa River delta just downstream.

Ski trails follow the top of the bluff and offer a moving panorama of the river valley below. Except during the most severe cold snaps there are stretches of open water on Lake Pepin that allow bald eagles to spend the winter. Bring a pair of binoculars and watch for the large birds gliding below or perched in large trees near the shoreline.

While you can drive to the top of the bluff, you'll certainly want to earn the fun downhill return run by skiing up the ravine. Another trail follows the valley floor around the historic town of Frontenac to Sand Point and a water-level view of the big river.

A freestyle 15-kilometer ski race is held at Frontenac the last weekend in January each year to help celebrate the **Lake City Winter Fest**.

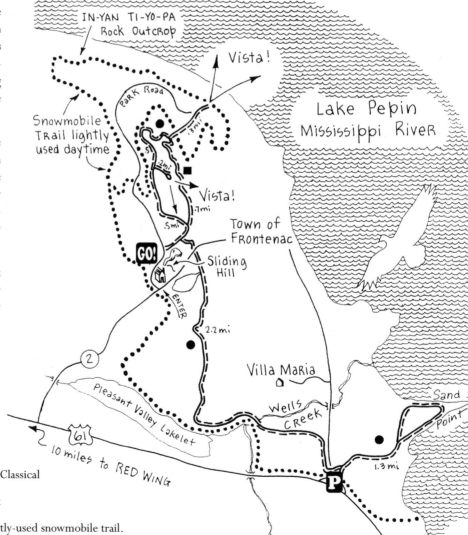

N

GO!   Trailhead. Parking.

- - - -   Combined Skating and Classical

◗   Easier   ⌁   More difficult

••••   Winter Walking on lightly-used snowmobile trail.

GATEWAY STATE TRAIL

Administered by Minnesota DNR   Phone 772-7935

GO! See map for trail access locations.   **Fee** Free, MN Ski Pass required

Trackset 15.5 km (9.7 mi)   **Skate Ski** None   **Length** 18.1 mile corridor

Rating Flat, easy skiing. Trails groomed weekly.   **Hours** Daily, 24 hours

Amenities   Outdoor toilets at 55th Street, Highway 96, and Pine Point Park (page 69) trail accesses.

Outing Lodge at Pine Point (439-9747) often open for fine dining and more.

Winter Walking 8.9 mile paved path is plowed west of I-694. Parallel packed trail east of 694 (not the ski trail!) is also available for walking or riding horses, sleigh rides, etc.

The prettiest off-road path in the east metro area becomes a solitary skiing retreat when the snow flies. Walking, bicycling, sleigh rides and skiing all find their place.

As busy as the Gateway State Trail is in summer, it is almost completely abandoned with the first serious snowfall of the season. True, the diagonal tracks laid on a nearly level abandoned railway corridor are not the most dynamic in town if you crave downhill excitement. But this is gorgeous countryside and the surrounding landscape of oak wooded hillsides and intimate little lakes with nary a building to tarnish the view is all the more seductive under a mantle of snow.

The plowed, paved path west of I-694 now extends all the way to Cayuga Avenue and will eventually continue to the State Capitol. Walkers east of 694 should use the parallel path next to the ski trail (this is the equestrian trail) to avoid ruining the ski tracks. This trail is packed and shared with an occasional sleigh.

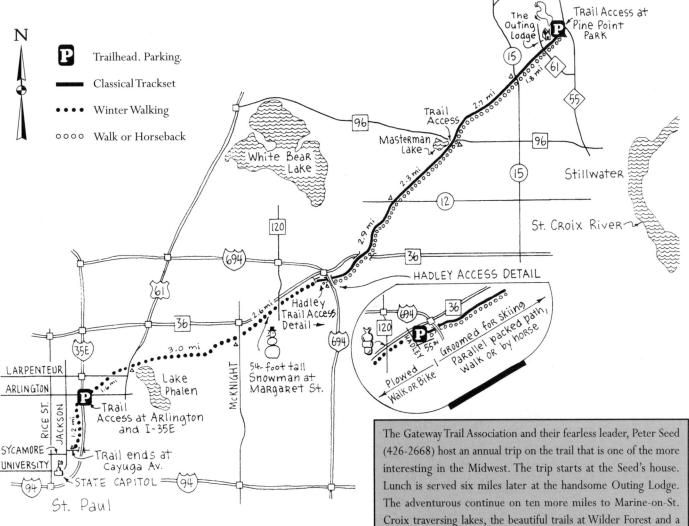

The Gateway Trail Association and their fearless leader, Peter Seed (426-2668) host an annual trip on the trail that is one of the more interesting in the Midwest. The trip starts at the Seed's house. Lunch is served six miles later at the handsome Outing Lodge. The adventurous continue on ten more miles to Marine-on-St. Croix traversing lakes, the beautiful trails at Wilder Forest and a long stretch along a marginally active railroad line!

23 HIDDEN FALLS – CROSBY FARM REGIONAL PARK

Administered by City of Saint Paul   Phone 266-6400

GO! There are three entrances: 1.) Mississippi River Blvd. and Magoffin, 1 mile south of Ford Bridge 2.) Shepard and Gannon Rds. 1 block east of Hwy. 5 (Seventh St.), 3.) Elway St. and Shepard Rd. 1 block west of I-35E.

Trackset 13 km (8 mi)

Rating Flat and easy

Hours 6 a.m. to 9 p.m.

Winter Walking 2 miles plowed, paved along Mississippi River Blvd.

Size 729 acres

Easy, secluded skiing along the beautiful Mississippi River.

The Mississippi River is an endless fascination. I have watched as a huge cottonwood tree, uprooted by a flood, drifted by like some strange, abandoned battleship. Bald eagles occasionally soar overhead. And late in winter, as the river breaks up, sheets of ice 100-feet-long glide by in the dark waters.

Having grown up around Chicago I am always impressed with how quick and easy it is to get to a natural setting in the Twin Cities. Entering the park you drop several stories down below the bluffs, leaving the manicured lawns and well-appointed houses far behind. Because of the relative isolation, you may feel more comfortable skiing with a friend.

This isn't wilderness but it is powerfully attractive. Huge cottonwoods, sheer sandstone cliffs, a spring-fed lake and the mighty Mississippi make this a place you could ski every day without tiring of it.

Hidden Falls can be found on the upstream end of the park near Magoffin. It is not on the ski trail, but the beautiful WPA-era stonework now framing the falls is worth searching out. Thomas Crosby staked out a farmstead near Crosby Lake in 1858 — the same year Minnesota became a state. The land was farmed until 1962 when it became a park.

HIGHLAND NINE HOLE SKI AREA

GO! Take Snelling Av. 2.3 miles south from I-94. **Sledding hill** next to blue water tower. Ski area is on Montreal.

Trackset 3 km (2 mi)

Rating Beginner to intermediate

Skate Ski Same length

Size 300 acres

This is an open course with some nice groupings of mature conifers and deciduous trees. There are some long views out across the Mississippi River Valley and the course has enough of a tilt to give beginners a thrill.

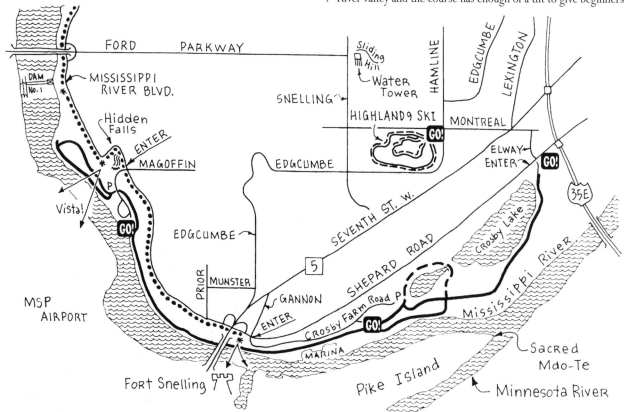

24 HOFFMAN HILLS STATE RECREATION AREA, WIS.

Administered by Wisconsin DNR   Phone 715-232-1242

GO! Take I-94 58 miles east to Co. Rd. B exit (first exit east of Menomonie). Go left (north) less than a mile to Rusk Road and turn right (east). Rusk becomes Co. Rd. E., turns left then right. About .3 miles past the right take a left (north) on Valley Road. Follow Valley as it curves and at the T-intersection turn right into park.

Trackset 14.7 km (9.1 mi)   **Skate Ski** Same length   **Size** 705 acres

Rating Big hills are the big draw but there's also 2.7 kilometers of easy skiing.   **Hours** Sunrise to sunset

Warming House Shelter with fireplace and wood. Outdoor toilet.   **Fee** $3 daily, $10 annual pass

Sledding Hill Steep, unofficial and located on south side of parking lot.

Winter Walking and Snowshoeing New mile-long trail through prairie and wetlands.

A classic day trip for good skiers, with exciting terrain, well-groomed trails and a great picnic spot next to the observation tower.

Hoffman Hills is just the ticket if you're bored with Murphy, Lebanon Hills and Afton, and need to explore new territory. It is about an hour east of the Twin Cities — a scenic cruise at 65 miles-per-hour and worth the trip.

The rugged hills offer great skiing and panoramic vistas from the ridgetops. A maturing forest covers the park with planted pines, birch, maple and oak.

Wildlife is abundant and the local ranger reports plenty of fox, coyotes, grouse, turkeys and woodpeckers. A bear was even spotted ambling through a while back.

A good approach with a group is to let folks explore for a couple of hours and schedule a lunchtime rendezvous at the picnic tables next to the observation tower. Though the tower stairs aren't maintained in winter, careful climbers will be rewarded with a grand view of the surrounding countryside. On windy days you may prefer the picnic shelter and a roaring fire as your rest stop.

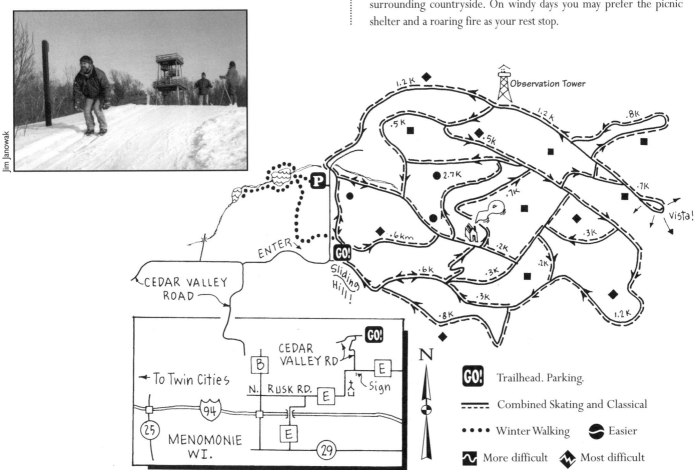

GO! Trailhead. Parking.

———— Combined Skating and Classical

•••• Winter Walking   ◐ Easier

〰 More difficult   ◆ Most difficult

Admin. by Hennepin Parks, Phone 941-4362, Richardson Nature Center 941-7993

GO! Exit 494 at Hwy 100-Normandale Blvd. and go south on Normandale .5 miles to 84th St. Turn right (west) and go one mile (road becomes Bush Lake Rd. and curves left) to RICHARDSON NATURE CENTER on left. Proceed one more mile to HYLAND LAKE PARK entrance on left.

Trackset 9.8 km (15.6 mi)   **Skate Ski** Same length   **Size** 1,000 acres

Rating Meticulously groomed trails for all skiers with some good hills

Fee Park permit ($4/day, $25/year)   **Hours** Sunrise to sunset

Warming House Visitors Center (open 10 to 5 weekdays, 9 to 5 weekends) is a handsome structure with a fireplace in Lakeview Room. Washroom, better food, gift shop and both **skate ski** and **no-wax ski rental.**

Sledding Hill Near Visitor Center   **Winter Walking** Packed 2-mile trail

Snowshoeing Trails and rental at Richardson Nature Center (below)

This area has superb winter sports facilities for cross country and downhill skiing, sledding, snowshoeing and ski jumping!

The first cross country ski trail in the Twin Cities was cut near the old Bush Lake ski jump in the winter of 1965–66. Thirty years later Hyland Lake is one of the finest cross country facilities in the area. It is also one of the most popular, so come for the camaraderie, not the solitude.

In 1998, an expanded five-kilometer lit trail will be operational. Check out the chapters on SKI JUMPING and DOWNHILL SKIING to discover the full range of winter sports available in this area.

RICHARDSON NATURE CENTER

A separate entrance (or ski here!) takes you into the nature center reserve. The deer watching programs (Tuesday and Saturday at 5 p.m.) are among the most popular of the many naturalist-led programs offered here. There are three miles of walking and snowshoeing trails (rental equipment available) to be enjoyed.

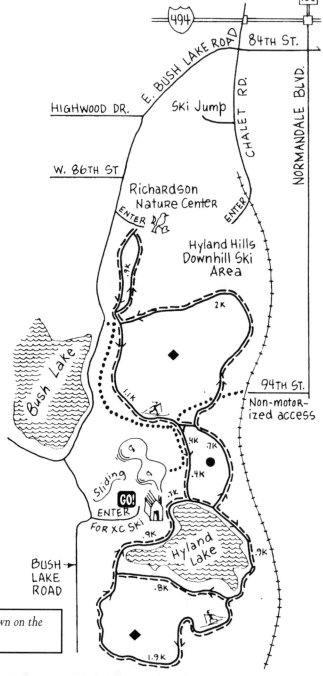

N

GO! Trailhead. Parking.

----- Combined Skating and Classical

•••• Winter Walking

● Easier   ⬧ Most difficult

Warming House (Visitor Center, etc.) as shown on the ski trail maps.

INTERSTATE PARK, WIS.

Administered by Wisconsin DNR   Phone 715-483-3747

GO! Take I-35 north 3.5 miles past where 35E and 35W join and exit on Hwy. 8 at Forest Lake. Go east on Hwy. 8 24 miles and cross the St. Croix River. Turn right (south) on Wis. Hwy. 35, go 1/4 mile and turn right again into the park.

Trackset 17.8 km (11 mi)   **Skate Ski** None   **Size** 1,400 acres

Rating Two hillier trails – mostly easier. NOTE! Funding may limit grooming.

Fee Nonresident $7 day, $25 annual pass   **Hours** 6 a.m. to 11 p.m.

Ice Age Interpretive Center Open 8 to 4:30 Monday through Friday and 9 to 5 weekends. Film and displays on natural and glacial history of park. Fireplace, water and washrooms.

Snowshoeing Naturalist-led snowshoe hikes (snowshoes provided). Call for reservations and program information.

Winter Walking Allowed on 4 miles of paved roads. Stay off ski trails.

> *W*isconsin's oldest state park rises above the spectacular Dalles of the St. Croix River. Ski along the river or past isolated stands of century-old pines.

St. Paul steamboat agent George Hazzard, responding to a threat that could have destroyed the rocky Dalles (to help pave Seventh Street!) mobilized forces that created America's first Interstate Park in 1895. The rugged beauty of this captivating canyon on the St. Croix is the result of complex geologic forces that included multiple lava flows over a billion years ago and the tremendous eroding force of a mighty river that drained Glacial Lake Duluth (Superior) 10,000 years ago.

Take the time to learn more about this fascinating story at the Ice Age Interpretive Center – it doubles as a convenient warming house. You'll also learn about the park's more recent natural history and about the vast forest of white pines that once covered this region.

Today's forest includes some of the best local remnants of old growth white pine to be seen. Additional highlights include river overlooks (Point and Skyline trails), beaver ponds and rock outcrops (Beaver Dam Trail), an old wagon road and sandstone ruins (Silverbrook Trail), and a demanding climb to a ridge overlooking a steep wooded ravine (Bluff Trail).

Oh yes, did I mention the half dozen eagles that usually overwinter here?

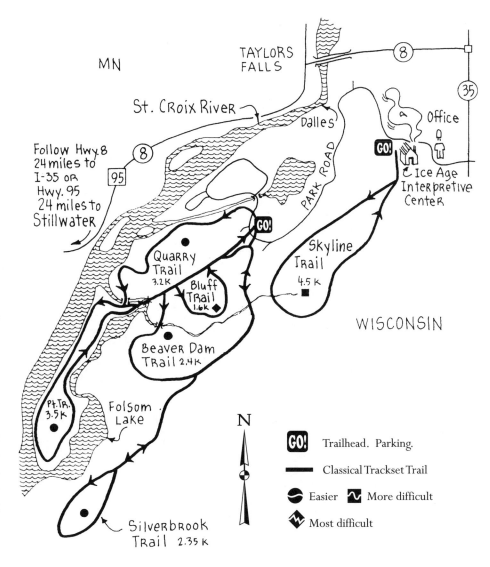

27 KINNICKINNICK STATE PARK, WISCONSIN

Administered by Wisconsin DNR   Phone 715-425-1129

Trackset 10.1 km (6.3 mi) Not groomed. Track often skied-in by ranger.

Rating Mostly easier but trail near sledding hill is very steep.

Fee Nonresident $7 daily, $25 annual   **Hours** 8 a.m. to sunset.

Winter Walking 2-mile park road   **Amenities** Outdoor toilet   **Sledding Hill** Yes

Size 1,242 acres

A great place to explore if you don't need groomed trails. Two beautiful blufftop overlooks, turkeys and eagles. Take care if skiing down along the river.

GO! Take I-94 east to Hudson. Take Exit 2 and turn right (south) onto Carmichael Rd. which becomes Hwy. F. Stay on F 8.7 miles. Turn right (west) on 820th Av. and go .2 miles to park entrance on left.

The Kinnickinnick (Ojibwa for a pipe smoking mixture that includes willow bark) provides some fine adventure skiing relatively close to home. While not groomed or trackset there were nice grooves on my visit laid by a previous skier and it was easy to get a good rhythm going. The sledding hill offers you the opportunity to try your telemark technique, but be careful on the adjacent trail where the park's two steepest downhills meet at the bottom of a ravine.

Enjoy one of the two fine vista points or venture down the steep trail that leads to the beach. Be very careful if you decide to ski out onto the St. Croix as there are springs along the shore and I saw a large stretch of open water on a visit after a solid week of below zero temperatures. The open water allows eagles to overwinter here and you may share my luck in watching one fly overhead.

The restored prairie is a pleasure to ski on a calm sunny day. Remnant native goat prairies cling to parts of the sheer, rocky Kinnickinnick River ravine. Watch for fox and turkeys along the park road and coyotes in the park's more remote stretches.

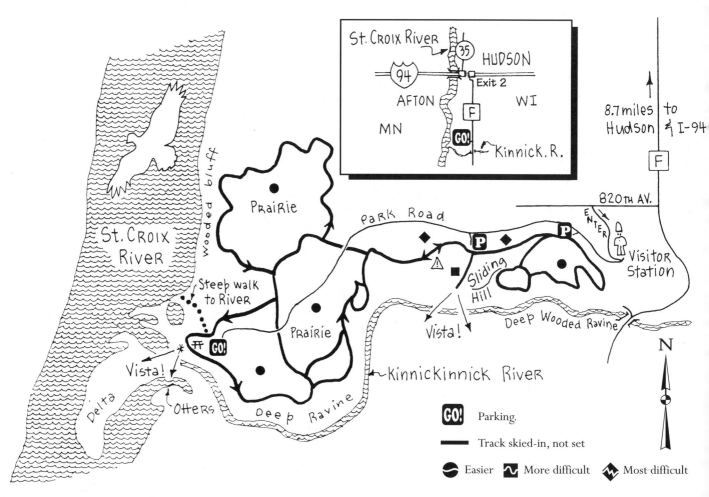

LAKE ELMO PARK RESERVE
SKI TRAILS

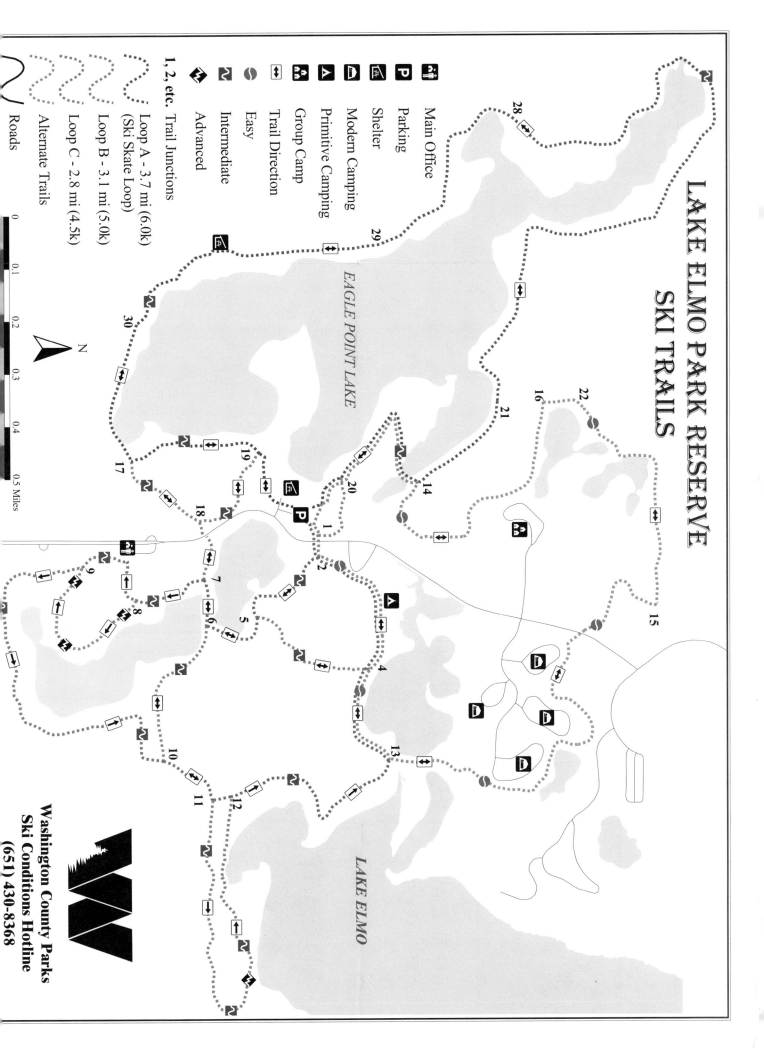

Main Office

Parking

Shelter

Modern Camping

Primitive Camping

Group Camp

Trail Direction

Easy

Intermediate

Advanced

1, 2, etc. Trail Junctions

Loop A - 3.7 mi (6.0k)

Loop B - 3.1 mi (5.0k)
(Ski Skate Loop)

Loop C - 2.8 mi (4.5k)

Alternate Trails

Roads

EAGLE POINT LAKE

LAKE ELMO

N

0   0.1   0.2   0.3   0.4   0.5 Miles

Washington County Parks
Ski Conditions Hotline
(651) 430-8368

Park Rules

For your safety and skiing enjoyment please observe these rules.

- ☐ Park in designated parking lots only.
- ☐ Ski during park hours only.
- ☐ Ski only on groomed trails.
- ☐ Observe directional signs.
- ☐ Ski skating allowed on loop A only.
- ☐ **No dogs or hiking on ski trails.**
- ☐ Possession or consumption of alcoholic beverages, including 3.2 beer, is prohibited.
- ☐ Snowshoeing is prohibited on ski trails.

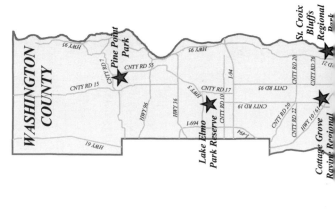

Fees

A **Washington County Parks vehicle permit** is required on all motorized vehicles. Permits can be purchased at the contact station or through the **Honor Box** when the office is closed.

Daily Permit	$ 5.00
Annual Permit	$ 20.00
2nd Annual Permit	$ 10.00

(Must be purchased at time of first annual for 2nd vehicle in your name)

The Washington County Park annual vehicle permit also provides admittance to Anoka and Carver County Parks.

Park Hours

7 a.m. to ½ hour after sunset.

MN Ski Pass

Washington County requires all cross-country skiers ages 16 and older to be licensed when skiing on Washington County ski trails. Daily or annual passes are available wherever DNR licenses are sold, Lake Elmo Park Reserve office and at Washington County License Centers.

Trail Grooming

The Washington County Parks Division grooms trails on a rotating schedule after a base of 6-8 inches is established.

Ski Trails at other Washington County Parks

Cottage Grove Ravine Regional Park (5.2 miles/8.4 km)
Pine Point Park (4.1 miles/6.6 km)
St. Croix Bluffs Regional Park (6.2 miles/9.9 km)

Ski Trails

10.8 miles of ski trails at Lake Elmo Park Reserve are groomed in this 2,165 acre park reserve. Three loops vary from easy to intermediate. As a park reserve, 80 percent of the area must be left in a natural state. Watch for wildlife, such as white-tailed deer, red fox, squirrels, rabbits and a multitude of birds.

Shelter

The ski shelter is located next to the ski parking lot. It includes picnic tables and a wood burning

Washington County Cross-Country Ski Trails

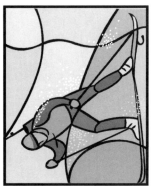

Lake Elmo Park Reserve

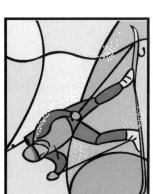

Washington County Parks

Division Office: 651-430-8370
Address: 1515 Keats Ave. N. Lake Elmo, MN 55042
www.co.washington.mn.us

Ski Conditions Hotline:
651-430-8368

E-mail:
parks@co.washington.mn.us

28 LAKE ELMO PARK RESERVE

Administered by Washington County   Phone 731-3851

GO! From St. Paul take I-94 east 5 miles and exit at Co. Rd. 19 (Keats Av.). Go left (north) 1 mile to park entrance.

Trackset 19 km (12 mi)   **Skate Ski** 6 km (3.7 mi)   **Size** 2,165 acres

Rating Well-groomed, beginner and intermediate level skiing

Fee County Pass ($4 day/$16 year), MN Ski Pass   **Hours** 7 a.m. to ½ hour after sunset

Warming House Heated with wood fire   **Toilet** Indoor and outdoor

Winter Walking Allowed on closed road (over 3 miles)

A huge expanse of lakes, woods and reclaimed farmland, with a good range of well-groomed trails for all levels of skiers including those who like to skate ski.

If you welcome the sound of coyotes howling in our increasingly urban metropolis, you will find this oasis of wild land to your liking.

As a designated park reserve Lake Elmo offers plenty of recreational opportunities while still meeting its mission for keeping 80 percent of the park in a natural state. The park is actively managed to increase habitat for wildlife. Wetlands have been reclaimed and prairie plantings are being seeded in.

The usual suspects — deer, fox, pheasants and hawks — can be seen on any given outing here. Visitors in the winter of 1996 enjoyed a special treat when a great grey owl, driven well south of its usual range by heavy snow, took up residence for a while.

Most of the trails at Lake Elmo are easy intermediate in difficulty. The casual skier will enjoy the forested trails in the middle of the park. The northern and western stretches of the park provide little natural cover and might be avoided when a stiff northerly wind is blowing.

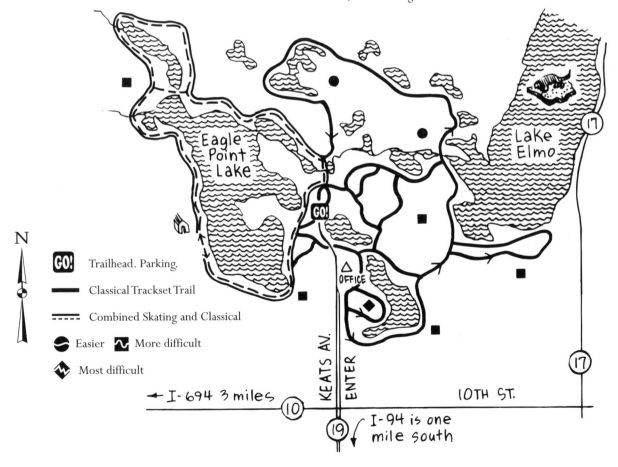

N

GO! Trailhead. Parking.

—— Classical Trackset Trail

----- Combined Skating and Classical

● Easier   ~ More difficult

◆ Most difficult

← I-694 3 miles   10TH ST.

KEATS AV.   ENTER   I-94 is one mile south

LAKE MARIA STATE PARK

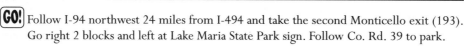

Administered by Minnesota DNR   Phone 878-2325

GO! Follow I-94 northwest 24 miles from I-494 and take the second Monticello exit (193). Go right 2 blocks and left at Lake Maria State Park sign. Follow Co. Rd. 39 to park.

Trackset 22 km (13.6 mi)   **Skate Ski** 5 km (3.1 mi)   **Size** 1,580 acres

Rating Hilly trails dominate north half, easier trails to south, well groomed

Fee $4 two-day, $20 annual pass, MN ski pass **Hours** 8 a.m. to 10 p.m.

Warming House Interpretive Center has washroom, water, sodas and candy.

Sledding Hill Big, steep hill – not groomed **Skating pond** Swept and lit at night

Camping Ski in to wood-heated cabin (reserve in advance) or 17 tent sites, each with table, fire ring and pit toilet.

Winter Walking and Snowshoeing Packed, 3-mile (round trip) trail

> *Peaceful skiing through one of the last remnants of the Big Woods. Sledding, nighttime skating and camping are visitor favorites.*

Early French explorers called this region of Minnesota the *Bois Grand,* or Big Woods, for the vast hardwood forest that covered the area. Old growth (over 150 years) maple and oak can still be seen along the trail, especially in the northern half of the park.

Lake Maria (pronounced ma-rye-uh) has great rolling hills for better skiers but even beginners will be able to negotiate several kilometers of trails in the southern half of the park. Ski lessons and a candlelight ski in late January are offered. Call for times.

A large deer herd roams the park, of course, but this is also excellent habitat for owls – barred owls, screech owls and great horned owls all nest in the park. By late February great horned owls can be seen guarding their nests, sometimes covered with snow, as they incubate their eggs.

Maple syrup starts to run by the end of March. This is the traditional end to the ski season and the park offers maple syrup hikes and programs to mark the occasion.

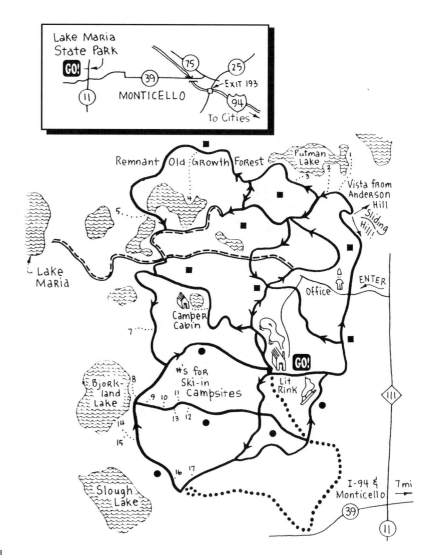

N

GO!   Trailhead. Parking.

━━━   Classical Trackset Trail

┅┅┅   Combined Skating and Classical

◓ Easier   〰 More difficult   ◆ Most difficult

•••• Winter Walking

LOUISVILLE SWAMP
and WILKIE UNIT-BLUE LAKE TRAIL

Administered by U.S. Fish and Wildlife Service, MN DNR Phone 335-2323

GO! To LOUISVILLE SWAMP take Hwy. 169 4.5 miles south of Shakopee and turn right (west) on 145th St. 1/2 mile to parking lot on left. To WILKIE take Hwy. 101 west about 1/4 from Hwy. 169 (old Co. Rd. 18) to poorly marked parking area on right (north) side of road.

Trails Not groomed or tracked. Free   **Hours** Sunrise to sunset

LOUISVILLE SWAMP

Trails Not groomed but track usually skied-in — 7 miles (11.2 km). State Trail is packed for snowmobiles and OK for walking and skate skiing. Use caution.

Rating Beginner to intermediate   **Size** 3,100 acres

Warming House The historic Jabs Farmstead has an original stone structure that has been renovated a bit to include a wood stove, firewood and some benches.

Camping One primitive site on river **Winter Walking** OK anywhere, stay off tracks

Historic Jabs Farm site.

Courtesy of Minnesota DNR

> *B*ig enough to get lost in, and remote enough to lose most of the crowds, Louisville Swamp is nearly as wild as it sounds.

The Minnesota Valley National Wildlife Refuge consists of several distinct units along the Minnesota River that will someday be linked with a continuous 80-mile trail from Fort Snelling to Le Sueur.

Louisville Swamp is one of my favorite getaways in metroland. It has a sense of vastness thanks to the 3-mile-wide valley carved 10,000 years ago by the Glacial River Warren, an aura of history highlighted by the 1860s stone farmsteads that remain, and the ability to surprise — whether it's the huge boulder you are sure to come upon or an unexpected vista across an untrammeled land.

WILKIE UNIT – BLUE LAKE TRAIL

Trail A 4.5 mile unimproved trail leads around Blue Lake.

Rating Almost completely flat. Unmarked.   **Size** 1,100 acres

Winter Walking OK anywhere, stay off tracks. No amenities.

> *A* heron rookery and muskrat houses are the marque billings on this little-used trail.

The Blue Lake Trail may be the least-visited place in this book. It is pretty tough to get lost, but you may feel more comfortable skiing or hiking with a friend.

An impressive 600-nest heron rookery (the heron have gone south) can be seen high in the cottonwood trees on the west side of Blue Lake. This area is closed to visitors during the spring and summer so that the great blue heron, great egrets and black-crowned night heron can nest in peace. The refuge naturalist leads at least one skiing or hiking trip to this area each winter. Phone 335-2323 for reservations.

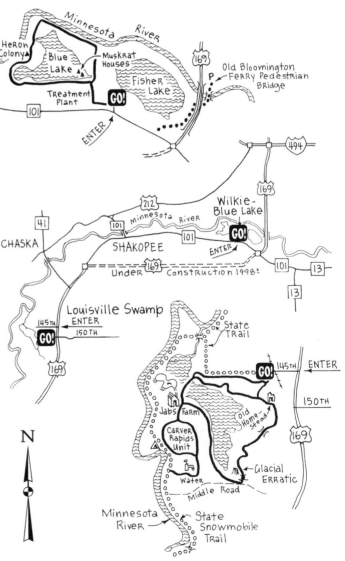

31 LEBANON HILLS REGIONAL PARK

Administered by Dakota County Parks Phone 438-4660 Trails Hotline 438-4671

GO! See maps for access and parking.

Trackset 21.1 km (13.1 mi)

Rating Well groomed, mostly intermediate level skiing

Fee Free, MN Ski Pass required

Skate Ski 4 km (2.5 mi)

Size 2,200 acres

Hours 5 a.m. to 11 p.m.

Warming House Diamond "T" Ranch (West Section – Phone 454-1464) is open daily 8 to 5 p.m. and has real food, washrooms, water, saddle stools, John Wayne, and **no-wax ski rental**. The Schultz Lake Shelter (east section) is open 9 to 5 on weekends only and has pop, hot chocolate, candy bars, water and washrooms.

Winter Walking A 9.2 mile (14.8 km) packed snow hiking trail (NOT the ski trail!) is maintained.

> *A vast natural refuge with a terrific trail system that remains relatively undiscovered in the fast growing southern suburbs. Heavily wooded with oak, maple, wild cherry and birch.*

Lebanon Hills is a superb area for the intermediate and more experienced skier. Though not quite as steep as Murphy Hanrehan, it still has plenty of hills plus the added advantage of longer level stretches to get a good stride going between climbs. Most of the trails are groomed for traditional skiing, but skate skiing trails are provided at the far western section of the park with access off of Johnny Cake Ridge Road.

The landscape at Lebanon Hills is typical of the rolling morainal country south of St. Paul. As the last glaciers retreated some ten thousand years ago they left huge blocks of ice strewn across the land. As these ice blocks melted they helped create the rolling knolls, small lakes, and sediment-filled marshes found at Lebanon Hills today.

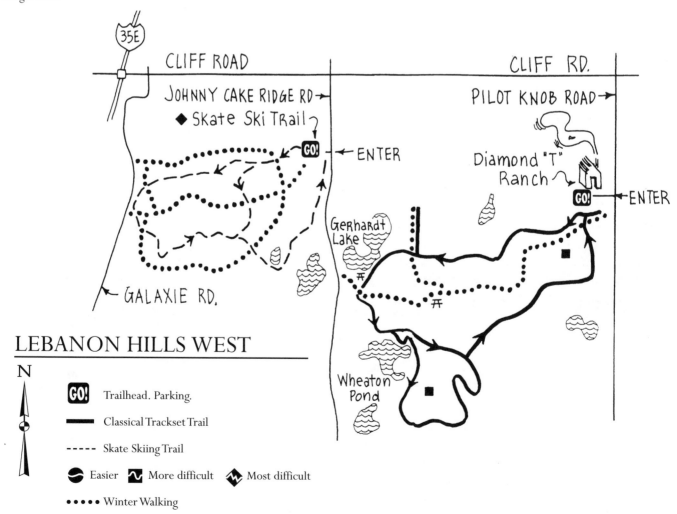

LEBANON HILLS WEST

N

GO! Trailhead. Parking.

——— Classical Trackset Trail

- - - - - Skate Skiing Trail

● Easier 〰 More difficult ◆ Most difficult

••••• Winter Walking

31 DAKOTA TRAILS – LEBANON HILLS EAST

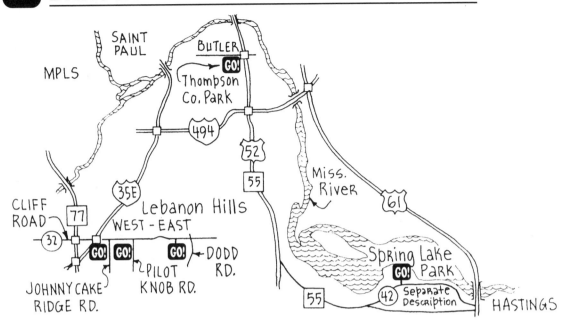

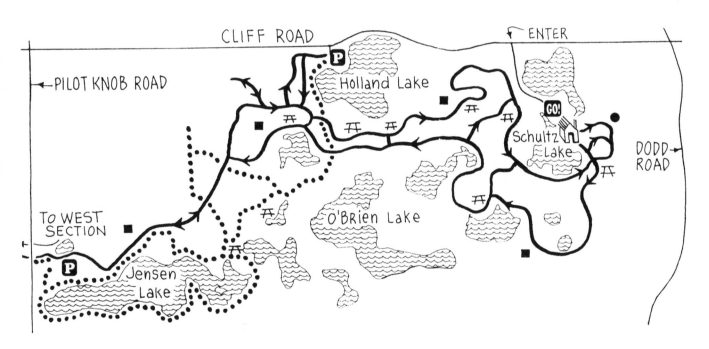

THOMPSON COUNTY PARK

Packed Trail (Skate Ski) 2.7 km (1.7 mi)

Winter Walking OK

Size 57 acres

Amenities Outdoor toilet

A vest-pocket ski park with some nice stands of oaks and a couple of good hills. Groomed for skate skiing.

A fine little park with just enough woods and hills to make it interesting if you live nearby. The start of the Kaposia Ravine has an intimate feel and a trail will soon circle Thompson Lake. So stop on by if you're in the neighborhood.

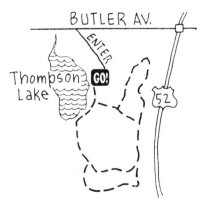

32 MILLE LACS KATHIO STATE PARK

Administered by Minnesota DNR   Phone 320-532-3523

GO! Take Hwy. 169 about 70 miles north from I-94 and then left on Co. Rd. 26 1 mile to park entrance on right.

Trackset 32.1 km (20 mi)   **Size** Over 10,500 acres

Rating There are plenty of trails for all abilities and excellent hills for experts.

Fee $4 two-day or $20 annual pass, MN Ski Pass   **Hours** 8 a.m. to 10 p.m. Office open 8 a.m. to 4:30 p.m.

Warming House Trail Center has fireplace, washrooms, tables, water, sodas. **No-wax ski rental** at office.

Sledding Hill North side of Trail Center   **Camping** Ski-in campsite, water and toilet

Snowshoeing Naturalist-led trips on special winter-only trails, moonlight trips and **rental snowshoes.**

Minnesota's fourth largest state park offers a wealth of winter delights — great cross country skiing, naturalist-led snowshoeing adventures and a sliding hill for the youngsters.

This land, where the Rum River flows out of Mille Lacs Lake has been inhabited for over 4,000 years. The Dakota and then the Ojibwa lived off the rich bounty of fish, waterfowl and the lush growth of wild rice in Ogechie Lake. Several archaeological sites are located within the park and the entire spectrum of ancient Native American culture can be seen at the Interpretive Center. The **MILLE LACS INDIAN MUSEUM** that opened in 1996 chronicles the history of the Mille Lacs Ojibwa.

The park has long served as a magnet for traditional skiers who enjoy the steep downhill pitches. The hills are part of a terminal moraine formed at the end of a glacial advance. While the vast pinery is long gone, a second growth forest covers most of the park along with a few isolated stands of conifers and a spruce tamarack bog that follows the Rum River.

Sharp observers may spot porcupines up in the trees or bobcat and fisher tracks in the snow. There are twelve types of bird feeders outside the Interpretive Center where evening grosbeaks, redpolls and goldfinches are regular visitors.

MINNEAPOLIS TRAILS

Administered by City of Minneapolis   Phone 661-4800

GO! See maps. WIRTH PARK **53** described separately. Trails described under **Winter Walking** are easily found with a city map that is also helpful in locating CEDAR LAKE TRAIL which is accessed at Glenwood and 12th St. in downtown, off Kenwood Pkwy. below Morgan Av., and at Cedar Lake Road and Ewing. GROSS GOLF COURSE located at 2201 St. Anthony Blvd.

Fee Free, MN Ski Pass required

Hours Sunrise to 10 p.m.

Skating Neighborhood rinks abound

Sledding Wirth, Columbia and Powderhorn Park

Winter Walking Over 26 miles of multiple-use paths are shoveled or swept daily. Bicyclists and skaters must yield to pedestrians. Cedar Lake Trail, Lake of the Isles, Lake Calhoun, Lake Harriet, Minnehaha Creek, Lake Nokomis and West River Road paths are open 24 hours daily.

> *Columbia, Gross and Hiawatha golf courses are pleasant enough ski trails but far more people enjoy winter walking, running, and biking on the meticulously cleared paths.*

COLUMBIA GOLF COURSE

Clubhouse phone is 789-2627

Trackset 4.8 km (3 mi)   **Size** 183 acres

Warming House Clubhouse open 9 to 5 weekends with snacks, sodas, washrooms and **no-wax ski rental**.

Sliding Hill Popular, 50-foot-high hill

Challenging golf course skiing. Acquired 400 years (1892) after Columbus set foot on what he hoped was India. Columbia is northeast Minneapolis's largest and perhaps least used (in winter) park. The mature oaks and skyline view (southeast corner) are park highlights.

HIAWATHA GOLF COURSE

Clubhouse phone is 724-7715

Trackset 3.2 km (2 mi)   **Size** 234 acres

Warming House Clubhouse open 9 to 5 weekends with snacks, sodas, hot drinks, washrooms and **no-wax ski rental**.

Rejected as a "desolate swamp" when first considered for park acquisition, the wild rice paddies have long since been cleared and filled for the golf course. Add snow, shake well, and strap on your skis.

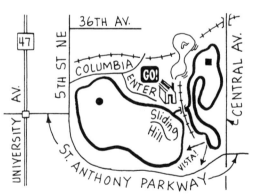

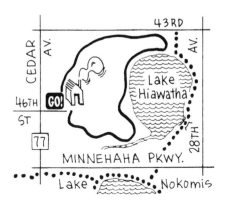

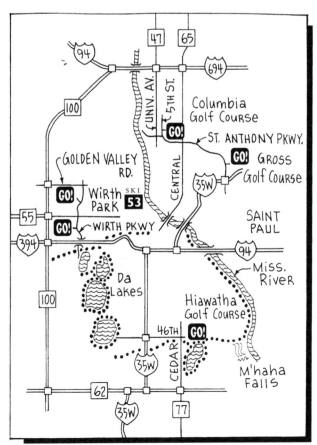

Administered by State of Minnesota   Phone 443-2460

GO! Take Hwy. 5 nine miles west of I-494 to entrance on left.

Trackset 9.6 km (6 mi)   **Skate Ski** None   **Size** 935 acres

Rating Moderate in difficulty. Green Heron Pond loop is easier.

Fee $4 adults, $1 ages 6-15, MN Ski Pass   **Hours** 8 a.m. to 4:30 p.m. weekdays, 11 a.m. to 4:30 p.m. weekends

Warming House The handsome Snyder Building has displays, water, washrooms and the delightful Tearoom that serves light lunches and deserts from 11:30 to 1:30 daily.

Winter Walking Three Mile Drive is plowed and cars are not allowed.

A pleasant escape for winter walking and skiing with the most civilized Tearoom available for aprés ski refreshments.

Stripped bare of flowers and foliage, the winter hardy trees and shrubs of Minnesota can be appreciated in their skeletal beauty on a bright winter day at the Arboretum. The colors and textures of tree trunks are often as distinctive as their individual leaf patterns and, of course, the Arboretum has a fine selection of pines, firs and spruce.

The terrain is quite rugged and includes the highest point in Carver County. The downtown Minneapolis skyline – 18 miles away – can be seen from here on a clear day. Beginners will probably want to stick to the loop around Green Heron Pond. And when the winds are really whipping most everyone will be more comfortable on the Forest Trails in the eastern half of the preserve.

Winter walking is almost as popular as skiing and everybody enjoys watching the bird feeders while partaking of some coffee and cake.

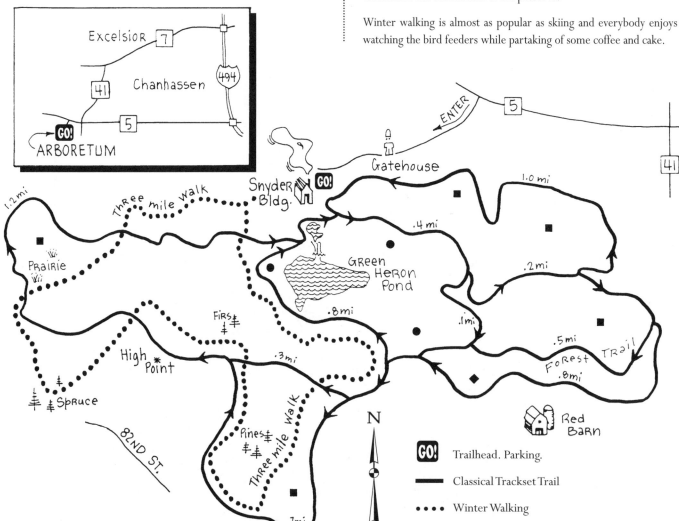

MINNESOTA ZOO

Administered by State of Minnesota   Zoo Hotline 432-9000, Ski Center 431-9308

GO! Take Hwy. 77 (Cedar Av.) south 8 miles from I-494 and follow large brown zoo signs to entrance.

Trackset 10 km (6.2 mi)   **Skate Ski** None   **Size** 485 acres

Rating One easy loop, lots of hills, regularly groomed.

Fee Zoo entrance – $8 adults, $4 ages 3-12   **Hours** 9 a.m. to 4 p.m. daily

Warming House The 1.5 acre Tropics Trail is more than just the largest warming house in the world — it's a wondrous winter escape into a world of gibbons, hornbills and clouded leopards. The nearby restaurant has soups, burgers and more. **No wax ski rental** and lessons on request.

Winter Walking Check out the Siberian tigers, camels, moose and rare Chinese takin — all denizens of winter — on the 3/4 mile Northern Trail.

Well, sure, these are the best ski trails in the Twin Cities (the world?!) to see wildlife. The trail system and support services are top-notch as well.

The Minnesota Zoo is built on a glacial moraine. This means hills abound. Nevertheless, this is likely the most popular place in the metro area for first-time skiers. There are 200 pairs of rental skis and on a nice weekend day they might all be checked out. Beginners can receive some simple instructions (like learning how to fall) and the trails are well-staffed on busy days with a volunteer ski patrol. Still, in the Zoo's own words "our ski trails can get a little hairy."

More experienced skiers will enjoy the rolling terrain and the chance to see large parcels of the zoo not accessible any other way. And what a thrill it is to gaze out on North America's largest captive herd of musk oxen, watch the snow monkeys cavort on even the coldest days and view trumpeter swans in the open water of the aerated pond.

The Minnesota Zoo is nationally acclaimed for its balance of research and conservation efforts with family entertainment. Here's your chance to add a good workout to the mix.

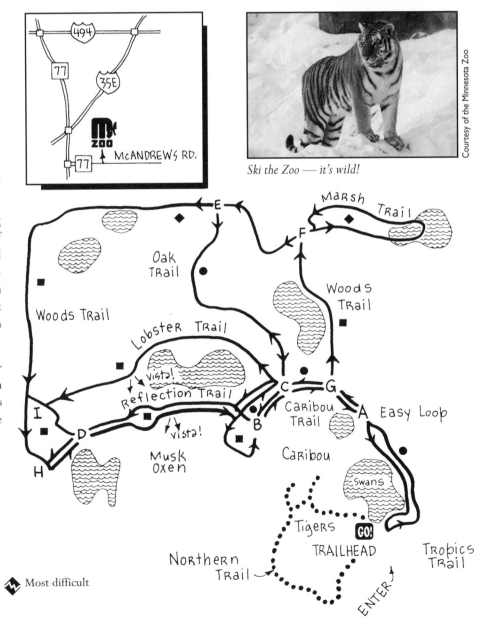

Ski the Zoo — it's wild!

Courtesy of the Minnesota Zoo

GO!   Trailhead. Parking.

──────   Classical Trackset Trail

● Easier   ⚡ More difficult   ◆ Most difficult

• • • • Winter Walking

MINNETONKA TRAILS

Administered by City of Minnetonka   Phone 988-8400

GO! See map for specific park locations. Hennepin Parks (559-9000) has a detailed map of
LRT TRAILS that are snow packed for winter walking, snowshoeing, skiing, etc.

Trackset 16.5 km (10 mi) total   **Skate Ski** None   **Grooming** Fridays

Winter Walking Over 32 miles of plowed, paved walking trails   **Hours** Sunrise to 10 p.m.

> *The Minnetonka Loop trail system will eventually link the entire city. Lone Lake and Purgatory Park are attractive enough to be regional draws for skiers.*

BIG WILLOW PARK

Trackset 1.6 km (1 mi)   **Size** 92 acres

Rating Easier   **Washroom** Indoors

Named for the largest darn willow you've ever seen (24 feet in circumference!) – Big Willow Park offers a good sampling of woods, water and wildlife. Minnehaha Creek runs through the middle of the park. The namesake willow is found on the west side of the large marsh.

HOPKINS HIGH SCHOOL

Trackset .8 km (.5 mi)   **Rating** Intermediate

This short trail is located directly across Lindbergh Drive from the high school. It is primarily used by students and the school ski team. It is groomed by the Minnetonka Parks department and has the added distinction of being the only place described in this book that I have not (yet!) skied.

LONE LAKE PARK

Trackset 4 km (2.5 mi)   **Size** 104 acres

Rating Intermediate or better   **Washroom** Indoors

A city park with regional appeal. Lone Lake has a great little trail that offers a bit of everything for the better skier – lakeside skiing, big curving downhills through the woods, marshes to race along and a big view to downtown from the southernmost hill. A new paved path is plowed for winter walkers.

MEADOW PARK

Trackset 3 km (1.8 mi)   **Size** 61 acres

Rating Easier   **Skating Rink** Lit, portapotty

Warming House Weekdays 4:30 to 10 p.m.,
    weekends, noon to 10 p.m.

When that heavy snow drops in late March do *not* head for Meadow Park for one last spin – unless you're good at water-skiing without a tow rope. About half of the trail is set along a cattail swamp and is usually mush by early spring. Beginners will appreciate the inherent flatness of Meadow Park and the surrounding oak covered knolls hide many of the houses. This is Minnetonka's best park in which to see deer.

PURGATORY CREEK PARK

Trackset 3.3 km (2.1 mi)   **Size** 140 acres

Rating Half are easier and half more challenging

Minnetonka's biggest park rivals Lone Lake for natural beauty and good skiing. Purgatory Creek wanders through a wide bowl of marshland before running into an oak-covered ridge that pushes it eastward. There are some nice views from the high spots and one hairy run down to the creek bridge.

VICTORIA – EVERGREEN PARK

Trackset 1.3 km (.8 mi)   **Size** 24 acres

Rating Easier

A small, neighborhood park with some quiet woods in a residential setting. The trail rolls gently.

STARING LAKE PARK

City of Eden Prairie   Phone 949-8442

Trackset 2.5 km (1.5 mi)   **Size** 160 acres

Rating Easier, groomed with new snow

Warming House Park shelter at main entrance has indoor and outdoor fireplaces, washrooms, pop and water. Open Sunday through Thursday till 9 p.m., Friday and Saturday till 10 p.m. **Outdoor Center** open noon to 5 p.m. Monday to Thursday and for programs on weekends.

Sledding Lit, groomed hill with free tubes

Skating Yes   **Winter Walking** 2.5 miles plowed

> *Eden Prairie's winter wonderland has something for everyone and one of the best sliding hills around.*

The plowed, paved path around Staring Lake is a boon to nearby residents, but it is the 700-foot-long sledding hill that is the big draw. Some 500 people might show up on weekends to laugh their troubles away on the big lit slopes. Skiing is pretty tame, but I spent a couple of hours following frozen Purgatory Creek downstream and had a fine time.

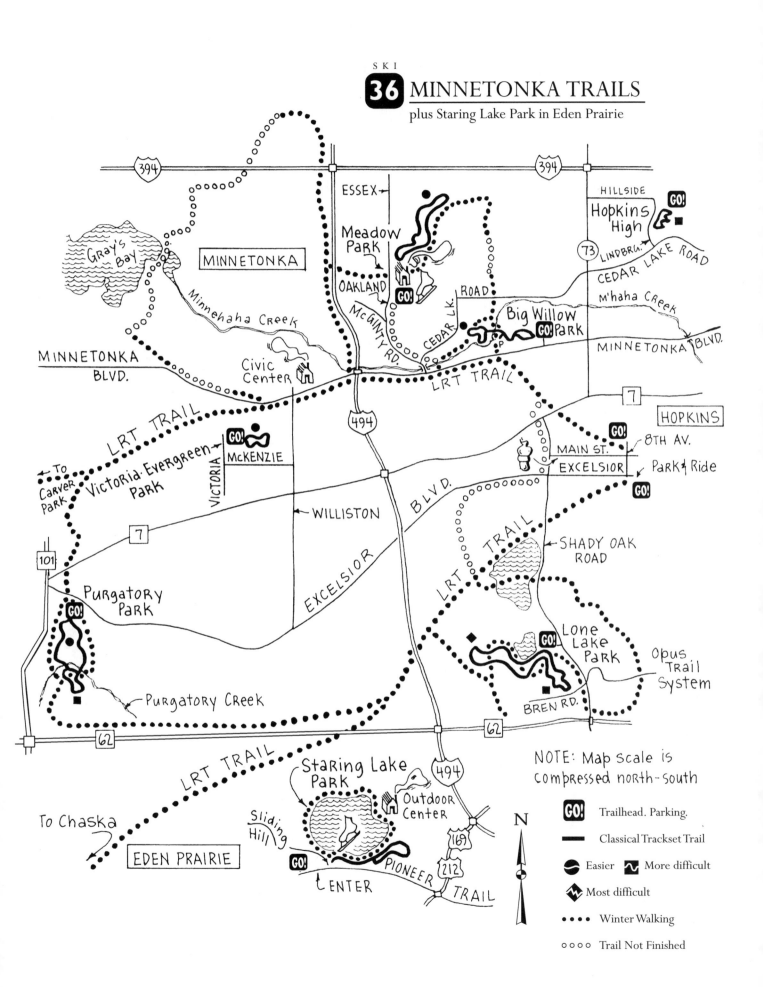

SKI
36 MINNETONKA TRAILS
plus Staring Lake Park in Eden Prairie

SKI 37 MURPHY-HANREHAN PARK RESERVE

Administered by Hennepin Parks   Phone 447-6913   Trails Hotline 559-6778

GO! Take I-35W (8.2 miles) to I-35E (10.2 miles) south from I-494 to Co. Rd. 42. Go right (west) on 42 about 2 miles and turn left (south) on Burnsville Parkway. Proceed about 2 miles to Co. Rd. 75, go left (east) and immediately left again into park.

Trackset 19.4 km (12.1 mi)   **Skate Ski** Same length   **Size** 2,900 acres

Rating Well groomed, challenging trails for advanced skiers only

Fee Park permit ($4/day, $25/year), MN Ski Pass required   **Hours** Sunrise to sunset

Warming House Open weekends only, 9 a.m. to 5 p.m. Simple shelter heated with wood stove — limited snacks, pop and hot chocolate. Portapotty outdoors.

Winter Walking OK on 3.6 mile horse trail. Hilly with uneven surface.

> *Murphy-Hanrehan is one of the kingpins of the metropolitan park system. The rugged glacial terrain offers breathtaking excitement for good skiers.*

Years ago, one of the first stories I heard about cross country skiing at Murphy-Hanrehan was that it was so treacherous that every other weekend they carried somebody off on a stretcher. This proved to be a fictitious bit of folklore. A parks supervisor recently told me that they have had only four serious accidents in the last 15 years. Still, no one should underestimate the difficulty of skiing this area.

For the advanced skier the trails at Murphy-Hanrehan are as demanding — and exhilarating — as any in the upper Midwest. Skiers must negotiate a nonstop series of uphill climbs and downhill runs with very few level stretches to kick and glide. This is excellent training ground for the annual Birkebeiner ski race.

The unbroken hardwood forest is beautiful in winter, but this is *not* the place to go for solitude. With fresh snow, over 400 people will converge here on the weekend. High school ski teams often train on weekday afternoons. Then again, there is over 200 feet of elevation change, and if that doesn't get your adrenaline pumping, then maybe you should take up skydiving.

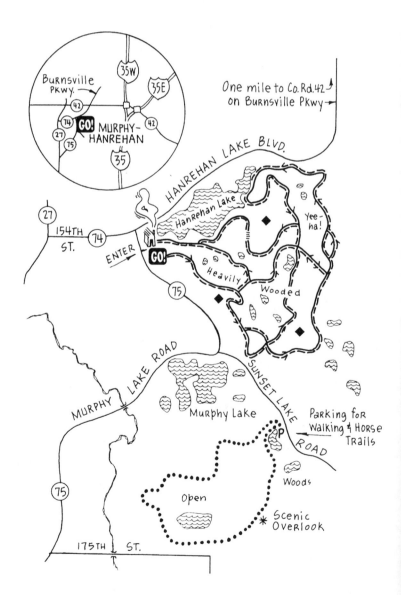

N

GO! Trailhead. Parking.

──── Combined Skating and Classical

•••• Winter Walking   ◆ Most difficult

SKI
38 NERSTRAND BIG WOODS STATE PARK

Administered by Minnesota DNR   Phone 507-334-8848

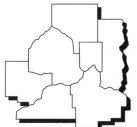

GO! Take I-35 south and exit at Hwy. 19. Go east into Northfield, cross the river, and in downtown take a right on Division St. Continue straight (south) as Division becomes Hwy. 246 and follow 246 to Co. Rd. 40. Turn right on 40 to park entrance on right.

Trackset 12.8 km (8 mi)   **Skate Ski** 4.5 mi packed track   **Size** 1,280 acres

Rating Intermediate skiing. Tracks are set but not groomed.

Fee $4 2-day, $20 annual pass   **Hours** 8 a.m. to 10 p.m.

Warming House Open 9 to 4 on weekends. Wood stove, table, washrooms and water.

Winter Walking The 5 miles of snowmobile trail south of Hwy. 40 are not often used for snowmobiling. Walking, snowshoeing and skate skiing are allowed on these packed-snow trails.

A quiet get-away through a hilly hardwood forest. Hidden Falls on Prairie Creek is a highlight.

Billed as "one of the last remnants of the Big Woods," Nerstrand harbors a large, mostly second growth, oasis of deciduous forest amidst the farmland of southern Minnesota. Many century-old maple, basswood and ash trees are sprinkled throughout the park. The continuous canopy assures that snow will stay longer and wind chill will not be a factor. The most recent glacier sent huge amounts of meltwater down Prairie Creek, carving the deep valley seen today. There are some long, thrilling downhill runs with over 140 feet in elevation change. These can be treacherous on ice (trails are not groomed), so call in advance for snow conditions. There are also plenty of relatively level areas where you can work up a good stride.

Hidden Falls is about 12 feet high and 90 feet wide. You need to take off your skis and walk down below to really appreciate this small cataract and its limestone walled glen. You may then wish to ski on down the frozen creek a ways before cutting back up to the trail that follows above. Explore Minnesota, to coin a phrase.

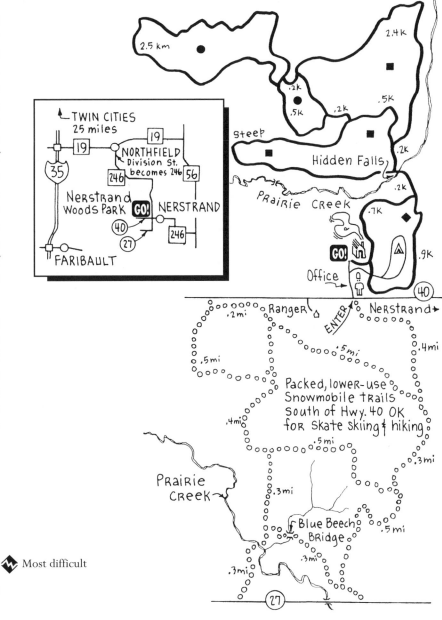

N

GO! Trailhead. Parking.

——— Classical Trackset Trail

● Easier   〰 More difficult   ◆ Most difficult

○ ○ ○ Shared Snowmobile Trails

SKI
39 PHALEN – KELLER REGIONAL PARK

Phalen Park is administered by City of St. Paul   Phone 266-6400   Chalet 778-0424
Keller Park is administered by Ramsey County   Phone 777-1707

GO! To **Phalen**: Take Wheelock Pkwy. east from I-35E 1.8 miles to entrance on left. To **Keller**: Take Wheelock 1.2 miles to Hwy. 61 (Arcade Street). Go left (north) 1.7 miles to Co. Rd. B. Go right 1 block to entrance on right.

Phalen Trackset 10 km (6.2 mi)   **Skate Ski** Same length   **Size** 494 acres

Keller Trackset 6.7 km (4.2 mi)   **Skate Ski** Same length   **Size** 103 acres

Rating Mostly beginner trails at Phalen. Keller approaches intermediate in difficulty.

Fee Free, MN Ski Pass required   **Hours** 6 a.m. to 11 p.m. (sunset at Keller)

Phalen Warming House Open 9 to 6 p.m. Sat., and 11 to 6 p.m. Sun. with food (hot dogs, donuts, fruit, etc.), washrooms and classic **no-wax ski rental**.

Winter Walking Plowed, paved 3 mile loop around Lake Phalen

Convenient golf course skiing, sledding and winter walking in a natural setting.

The ski trails at Phalen and Keller are joined together at the Winter Carnival for the 15-kilometer *King Boreas Ski Race*. This annual event draws 150 plus skiers and tends to be one of the rowdier races on the calendar.

Perhaps this is fitting as the park is named for Edward Phalen (also spelled Phelan) who made a land claim here during Minnesota's territorial days. A soldier discharged from Fort Snelling, he was imprisoned but released as a suspect in the city's first murder. In 1850, Phalen was indicted for perjury and fled west.

Keller and Phalen are part of a chain of lakes that mark the course of an ancient river much larger than today's Mississippi that carved its course during pre-glacial times. St. Paul acquired the land for $22,000 in 1899 to build a park.

Today Phalen Park is used for general skiing, high school races and *Hihtos* (Finnish for race) open to the public. Larger group events are more easily accommodated here than at Como due to the bigger clubhouse and longer ski course. Keller Park is less popular but a bit hillier and more scenic.

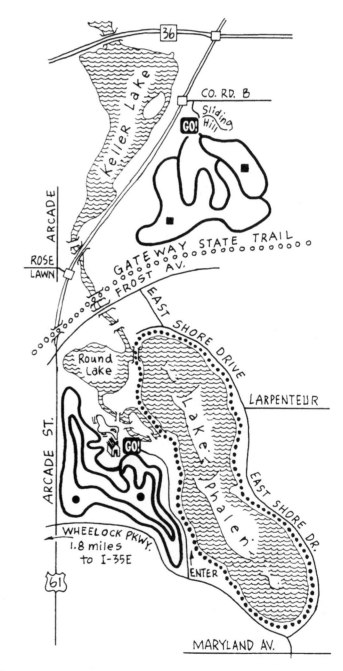

N

GO! Trailhead. Parking.

——— Combined Skating and Classical

◓ Easier   ⌁ More difficult

•••• Winter Walking

PINE POINT PARK

Administered by Washington County   Phone 731-3851

GO! From St. Paul take I-35E north to State Highway 36. Go east on Hwy. 36 12 miles to Manning Av. (Co. Rd. 15). Head north (left) on Manning 3 miles to Hwy. 96, then right (east) on 96 1.8 miles to Co. Rd. 55 (Norell Av.). Go left (north) 3 miles on 55 to park entrance on left. NOTE: To reach the **Outing Lodge** follow above but take a left on Myeron Rd. from Norell Av. about 2 miles north of 36. Proceed 1.2 miles to entrance on right.

Trackset 8 km (5 mi)   **Skate Ski** None   **Size** 296 acres

Rating Some intermediate level drops but better beginners should do fine

Fee County Pass ($4 day/$16 year), MN Ski Pass   **Hours** 7 a.m. to 1/2 hour after sunset

Warming House No   **Toilet** Outdoor   **Rental** No

Special The **Gateway State Trail** traversing the park is groomed for classical skiing. The **Outing Lodge at Pine Point** (reservations required, phone 439-9747) is a wonderful place to spend the night or enjoy a great meal.

> *A winter wonderland for classical cross country skiers. The Outing Lodge is a country inn with a European flavor and fine dining — well worth a visit.*

Under a mantle of snow, Pine Point Park is transformed into a scene of winter splendor. The forest of planted pines and spruce feels more like the northwoods than north Washington County. Skiers love the tunnels of pine-scented boughs that define this special place.

Pine Point Park is a major trailhead for the **Gateway State Trail** (see page 49). A shelter with indoor toilets is being built here. The trail is quite level as it passes through the park but offers some nice vantage points.

Lakes and pines offer the perfect backdrop for the **Outing Lodge at Pine Point**. This site was Minnesota's second "poor farm,"

founded in 1858 for indigents and those down on their luck. Today's bed and breakfast is a 1924 Georgian-style structure that has been transformed into a warm, inviting inn with wide-planked wooden floors and a huge fireplace topped by a ten-foot limestone mantel. Rooms start at $85 and all include a private bath, many with whirlpools.

Dinners are also special with several culinary outings featured every season. The Outing Lodge was selected in 1988 by Orion Films to recreate the lavish banquet features in the movie *Babette's Feast*. Presented just four times a year, reservations are required for this and other unique dinners that often revolve around a holiday.

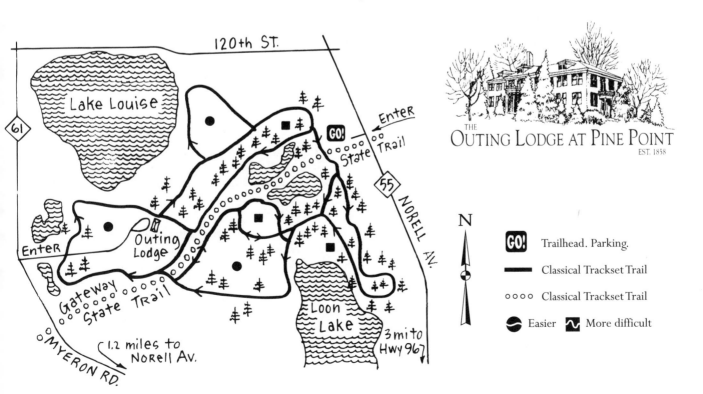

THE
OUTING LODGE AT PINE POINT
EST. 1858

GO! Trailhead. Parking.

——— Classical Trackset Trail

ooooo Classical Trackset Trail

● Easier   ∿ More difficult

41 PINE TREE APPLE ORCHARD

Privately run by the Jacobsons   Phone 429-7202

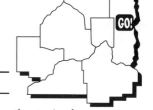

GO! Take Hwy. 61 four miles north of I-694 to Hwy 96. Turn right (east) and go 1.5 miles to Apple Orchard Road. Go left (north) and follow signs to entrance.

Trackset 10 km (6.2 mi)   **Skate Ski** Same length   **Size** 300 acres

Rating Intermediate level skiing. Tracks are set but not groomed.

Fee $2 per person   **Hours** Daily, 10 a.m. to 1/2 hour before sunset

Warming House Bake shop with eating area, washrooms and water

Country skiing with a hot apple pie chaser. A great place to go skiing with friends or family, especially if you like a few hills.

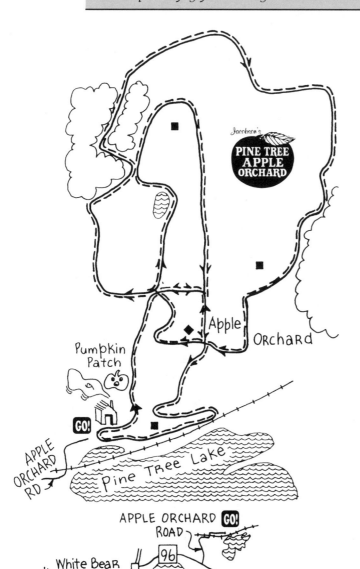

As you wind down narrow Apple Orchard Road the thought smiles upon you – you're in the country! While that big white bear is stuck watching traffic on Highway 61, you can relax and enjoy the day.

Set on rolling hills overlooking Pine Tree Lake, the apple orchard and farmstead offer a picturesque landscape for some fine ski touring. The orchard has been around since 1904, in the Jacobson family for almost 40 years and now includes 7,500 apple trees, strawberry fields and a pumpkin patch. The terrain is reasonably challenging and the family had some fun naming the trails – North Forty Trek, Cider Slide, Viking Run (experts only) and, best saved for last, Piece of Pie.

What could bring more pleasure after skiing on a crisp winter day than sitting down to some hot apple pie and fresh brewed coffee. If your grandma doesn't have a ski trail in her backyard, I heartily recommend a visit to Pine Tree Apple Orchard.

OAKDALE CITY PARK — map on next page

Administered by City of Oakdale   730-2702

Trackset 7.2 km (4.5 mi) tracked only, intermediate
Size 163 acres   **Fee** Free

Challenging skiing at one of the best city parks around. New nature center.

Warming House Nature center at 4444 Hadley Av.

A new nature center (call for hours) in an old farmhouse opened in June, 1996. This should spark some interest in this scenic and underused park. There are some nice stands of woods and good hills hidden away in here. The trails seem to go every which way but the park is not so big that you will stay lost for long.

Fee Free, MN Ski Pass required   **Hours** Sunrise to sunset

Facilities Sledding hills at Manitou Ridge and Snail Lake. Outdoor toilets only except at
Tamarack Nature Center. Long Lake Regional Park has 2 mile paved, plowed path.

SNAIL LAKE REGIONAL PARK
580 Snail Lake Blvd. Parking at beach, so. side Snail Lake

Trackset 2.4 km (1.5 mi) groomed (intermediate) plus
5 km (3 mi) of informal trails   **Size** 450 acres

> *A fine set of trails through woods and marsh.*

TAMARACK NATURE CENTER
(Phone 429-7787) • 5287 Otter Lake Road

Trackset 5 km (3.1 mi) easier and intermediate **Size** 335 acres

Warming House Nature Center open until 4:30 daily with washrooms, vending machines, **snowshoe** and **ski rental**.

Winter Walking 1.1 mile paved path

> *Ski, walk or snowshoe through a pleasant preserve.*

The clean, contemporary interpretive center has interactive displays, live animals and a full time naturalist. Groomed trails traverse a nice variety of prairie, woodland, evergreen plantation and marsh. Deer, fox and roosting owls may also be seen. A large tamarack bog once covered this land, but the rot-resistant trees were cut in 1917 for log home construction.

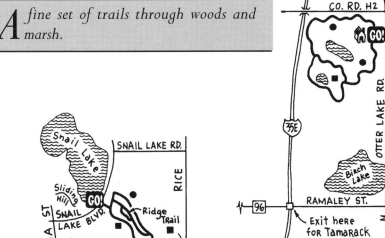

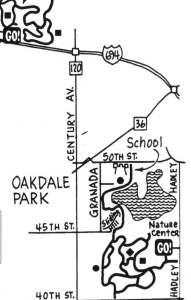

SNAIL LAKE PARK *continued*

A mature oak forest and 60-foot-high ridge define the official ski trail north of Gramsie Road. Thank Tom Rice and the North Star Ski Touring Club for the beautiful trails. Trail building is easy to take for granted until you spend a morning, like I did here, trying to plane a 4-foot-diameter tree stump down to level ground. (Hint – use a chainsaw.)

If snow conditions are good, you will definitely want to check out the narrow ungroomable trail along the top of the ridge for some thrills and chills. You may also take the underpass to the south side of Gramsie Road where an easier trail is often cut along the east side of Grass Lake.

MANITOU RIDGE GOLF COURSE
3200 N. McKnight Road

Trackset with skate ski 4.8 km
(3 mi) intermediate to advanced

> *Good grooming and big hills.*

Beautifully groomed trails for both traditional skiers and skaters. The course is kept in excellent shape for the high school meets that are held here. Manitou Ridge has some serious downhills and one hilltop has a view of both downtowns.

43 RED WING EAST END TRAILS

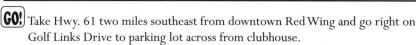

Administered by City of Red Wing   Phone 612-385-3674

GO! Take Hwy. 61 two miles southeast from downtown Red Wing and go right on Golf Links Drive to parking lot across from clubhouse.

Trackset 13.9 km (8.7 mi)   **Skate Ski** 8 km (5 mi)

Rating Blufftop trails are fast and narrow. Golf course is easier.

Fee Free, MN Ski Pass required   **Hours** Sunrise to 10:30 p.m.   **Size** 500 acres

Warming House The golf clubhouse is open daily from 9 a.m. to 5 p.m. and has snacks, water and washrooms.

Winter Walking Barn's Bluff is a spectacular hike before the snow falls or during a dry winter stretch. Be very careful as the trail can get icy and dangerous. Look for eagles as you gaze out on the Mississippi River.

One of Fred's Top Ten Metro Ski Areas. Spectacular views, challenging terrain and relative solitude make this place a winner.

It's not often you get a chance to watch bald eagles gliding 100 feet *below* where you're sitting. That's exactly the pleasure I had one sunny afternoon in January at the far north end of the Red Wing ski trails. Watch for an open field and a rock-walled corridor that leads to a view of Barn Bluff. The open water from here to past Colvill Park can allow a half dozen or more of the big birds to overwinter in this area.

It's quite a haul to ski to the top of Sorin's Bluff but well worth the effort. The narrow wooded trail hugs the bluff's edge and permits some great panoramas of the Mississippi Valley. A new skate skiing trail is being laid out on the open prairie up here to augment the combined trail on the Mississippi National Golf Course down below. I usually just tolerate golf course ski trails but the layout here was enticing enough for me to think twice about taking up golf again.

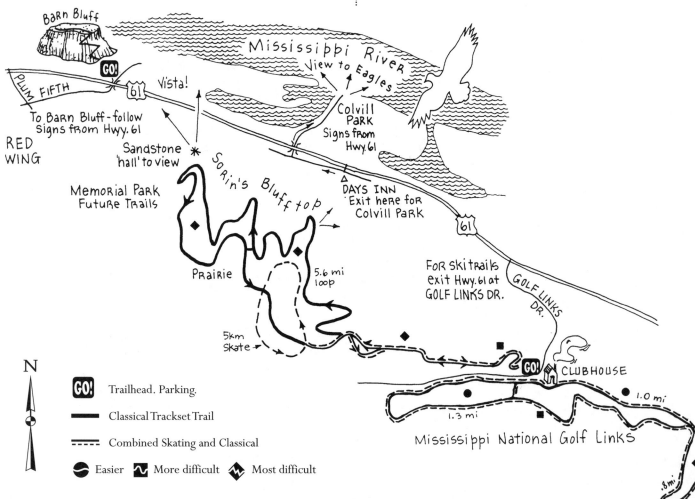

N

GO! Trailhead. Parking.

—— Classical Trackset Trail

---- Combined Skating and Classical

● Easier   ⌁ More difficult   ◆ Most difficult

WOOD LAKE NATURE CENTER

Trackset 4 km (2.5 mi) **Size** 150 acres

Rating Beginners **Hours** 5 a.m. to 11 p.m.

Warming House The nature center is open 8:30 to 5 Monday through Saturday and noon to 5 Sunday. Displays, touch-and-feel exhibits, live animals, washrooms, water and **no-wax ski rental.**

Snowshoeing On preregistered naturalist hikes only

Winter Walking 3-mile packed snow trail

Quality programming, wildlife, skiing and walking in a natural setting in the city.

A wide open marsh abutting a major freeway seems like an unlikely place to find an abundance of either skiers or wildlife, but Wood Lake must be the exception that proves the rule.

Nesting great horned owls, deer (of course) and three active fox dens (making this one of the easiest places to get within 20 feet of a wild fox) are part of the attraction. The center's close proximity to a large populace is certainly another good reason for its popularity.

But ultimately it is the active and imaginative programs that are Wood Lake's biggest draw. As conditions permit there is lantern skiing on Friday nights in January and February. Family snowshoe hikes, Quinzhee (snow shelter) building, fireside soup tales and a snowflea circus are among the many programs offered each winter. Stop on by.

RICH ACRES GOLF COURSE

Phone 861-9341

Trackset 6.5 km (4 mi) **Size** 120 acres

Rating Easier, slight roll to trail

Warming House Clubhouse open 9 to 5 daily with snacks, washrooms, water and **no-wax ski rental.**

Airplane buffs and locals enjoy the trail's close proximity to the international airport.

The Rich Acres Golf Course clubhouse is one of the last structures standing east of Cedar Avenue. By the year 2000 and perhaps earlier, the airport will move in as their planned expansion is realized.

Meanwhile, this is a great place to get some exercise while you watch the big birds zooming in and out of the airport. Count the rivets, wave to the pilot and ignore the fact that skiing is usually considered a silent sport.

N

GO! Trailhead. Parking.

- - - - Classical Trackset Trail

Easier

•••• Winter Walking

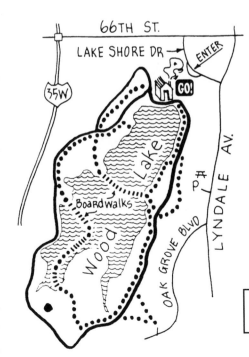

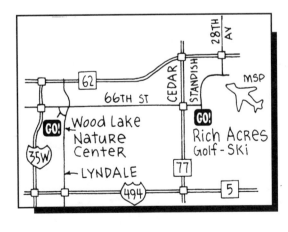

Warming House (Visitor Center, etc.) as shown on the ski trail maps.

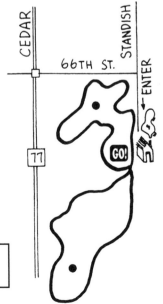

SKI 45 RITTER FARM PARK– LAKEVILLE

Administered by City of Lakeville   Phone 985-4400

GO! Take I-35 south 4 miles from junction of I-35E/I-35W to the 185th St. exit. Turn left, cross freeway and take an immediate right on Kenrick Av. (frontage road). One mile down take a right on 195th to entrance.

Trackset 12 km (7.5 mi)   **Skate Ski** Same length   **Size** 315 acres

Rating Intermediate skiing, groomed weekly   **Hours** Sunrise to sunset   **Amenities** Outdoor toilet

Fee Free, MN Ski Pass required

A beautifully designed network of challenging countryside trails.

Ritter Farm Park is located less than a mile from Murphy Hanrehan Park Reserve and enjoys the same rolling woods as its better known neighbor. Take a ride on the Matterhorn Trail and you'll be convinced.

During the mid- to late 1970s this was one of the premier areas in the state for cross country skiing. The Lakeville Ski Club gained easements for 50 kilometers of trails on nearly 1,000 acres of land, and the main loop was designed by a gentleman who had laid out courses for the Olympics. One memorable Citizens Tour drew almost 500 participants.

The glory days are gone, but in their wake lies a skiing experience that is quieter (40 people may show up on a nice weekend day now) and just as rewarding. Ritter Farm Park is endowed with almost every type of plant cover you will find in the metro area — apple orchards and pine groves, blue spruce and black walnut trees, corn fields and marshland. There are some nice sweeping vistas and the park's manager reports that badgers and pheasant can be found along with the usual deer and fox. An equestrian and snowmobile trail circle the park perimeter.

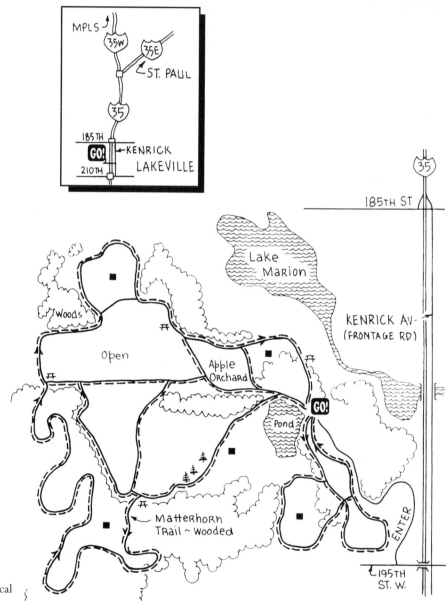

N

GO! Trailhead. Parking.

– – – – Combined Skating and Classical

● Easier   ∿ More difficult

ROSEVILLE TRAILS

Administered by City of Roseville   Phone 415-2100   Oval Phone 415-2160

Fee Free, MN Ski Pass required   **Hours** 8 a.m. to 10 p.m.
Ski Rental At the Activity Center on Arona, just south of Co. Rd. C2

Roseville is home to the John Rose Minnesota Oval — perhaps the finest public skating facility in the state. They also set tracks for cross country skiing at four parks and winter walking is popular around Lake Bennett.

ACORN PARK

Trackset 1.6 km (1 mi)   **Size** 36 acres
Rating Intermediate level
Amenities Skating rink, warming house, water, washrooms

An easy intermediate trail through the woods and fields where deer and fox occasionally roam. But for a real challenge, how 'bout a round of frisbee golf on skis at the championship course here.

CEDARHOLM GOLF COURSE

Trackset 1.9 km (1.2 mi)   **Size** 34 acres

Cross country ski lessons are offered here on weekends in December and January. Typical golf course skiing otherwise.

JOHN ROSE MINNESOTA OVAL

Phone 415-2160 for hours and events

Amenities Snacks, washroom and **ice skate rentals**

The Oval features the "largest artificial ice surface in North America." This is a splendid facility that hosts open public skating, speedskating races and Bandy (think hockey on a soccer-sized field of ice — no checking) championships.

CENTRAL PARK – BENNETT LAKE

Plowed Path 2 miles   **Size** 220 acres

Canada Geese and suburban strollers make the rounds at Bennett Lake. Geese and other waterfowl are drawn to the open, aerated lake. Winter walkers like the plowed, paved paths.

CENTRAL PARK – DALE STREET

Trackset 1.8 km (1.1 mi), 2 easy loops

HARRIET ALEXANDER NATURE CENTER

Phone 415-2161 for program information

Hours Tues. to Fri. 10 to 2, Sat 10 to 4, Sun. 1 to 4
Trail 2.4 km (1.5 mi) multiple use
Amenities Displays, live animals, washrooms and water

The most natural setting of any Roseville park is the perfect place for their interpretive center. Winter programs on hibernation (where did those bees go anyway?), winter birds and animal tracking plus snowshoeing, Norwegian kick sled and full moon hikes.

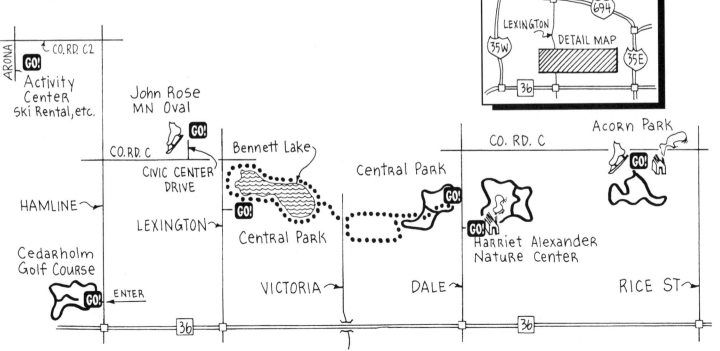

SHERBURNE REFUGE &
SAND DUNES STATE FOREST TRAILS

Sherburne National Wildlife Refuge, phone 612-389-3323 or 441-6010
Sand Dunes State Forest, phone 856-4826

Administration Sherburne National Wildlife Refuge is administered by the U.S. Fish & Wildlife Service (31,000 acres total). Sand Dunes State Forest is run by the Minnesota DNR.

Fees Free, MN Ski Pass required at Sand Dunes

Office Refuge Headquarters on Co. Rd. 9 open weekdays 8 to 4:30 p.m.

Hours Sunrise to sunset

SAND DUNES STATE FOREST

Trackset 7.4 km (4.6 mi)   **Size** 6,000 acres

Rating Easier to advanced skiing

> *A surprising landscape of sandy hills covered in native oak savanna and towering planted pines. Fun hills, few people.*

A planted grove of 50-foot-high Norway pines greets visitors to Sand Dunes State Forest. This is a beautiful landscape and not the first image you would connect with sand dunes.

Robert Orrock, the first white settler, arrived in 1857 when the land was virgin prairie and oak savanna. Newcomers farmed the marginal soils until the drought of 1933–34 when the worn out soils "took to the air and drifted like snow." By 1941, concerned citizens began experimental tree planting to help stabilize the shifting sands. And in 1943 a bill was passed that first established the state forest.

The campground and adjoining Uncas Dunes Scientific and Natural Area appear much like the presettlement prairie and oak savanna that once covered this area. An interpretive sign in the campground at Campsite 28 describes this native habitat.

MAHNOMEN TRAIL — Sherburne National Wildlife Refuge

Trail 3 miles, not tracked or groomed, outdoor toilet

Winter Walking OK, but stay off ski tracks

> *Another quiet retreat on a level trail with some almost indiscernible Indian Mounds.*

Mahnomen is an Ojibwa word for the wild rice that used to grow in abundance at Rice Lake. Archaeologists have located an ancient village on the north side of the lake that dates back several hundred years. A bit more wooded and even flatter than the Blue Hills Trail.

WOODLAND TRAIL — Sherburne N.W.R.

Trail 7.5 miles, untracked, windy and open

> *Park on the road, guaranteed solitude awaits.*

BLUE HILL TRAIL — Sherburne National Wildlife Refuge

Trackset 5.5 miles, untracked

Winter Walking No — use the Mahnomen Trail

> *Punctuated by the singular rise of the landmark Blue Hill, the namesake trail is a quiet, gentle escape.*

Blue Hill has been a landmark since long before the first white settlers arrived. The prominent, cone-shape hill was formed by glacial debris that collected in a deep depression in the huge slab of glacial ice. The 100-foot-high hill had three downhill ski runs in the early 1960s. Buck Lake just north of here is another glacial phenomena known as an ice block lake. Imagine the size of the glacial remnant that eventually melted to form this lake.

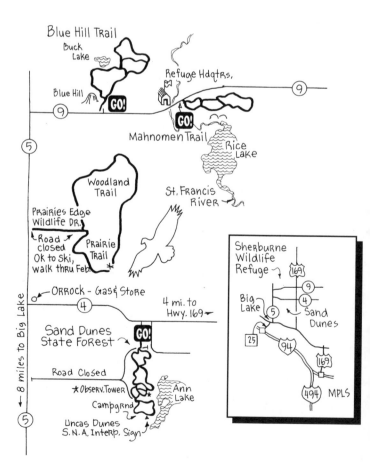

Administered by Dakota County Parks Phone 438-4660 Trails Hotline 438-4671

GO! Take Hwy. 52 8 miles south of I-494 and follow Hwy. 55 as it splits left (east) to Hastings. Go 4.5 miles and take Co. Rd. 42 left 2 miles to park entrance on left.

Trackset 5.8 km (3.6 mi)　　**Skate Ski** 1.6 km (1 mi)　　**Size** 975 acres

Rating Groomed. Rolling but beginner-friendly　　**Hours** 8 a.m. to sunset　　**Fee** Free, MN Ski Pass required

Amenities Heated washrooms, water and nearby archery trail　　**Snowshoeing** Archery Trail OK

Spectacular Mississippi River panoramas, solitude and silence.

On a sunny March afternoon there are few places I'd rather be than skiing the blufftops overlooking this big shining bend in the Mississippi River. Spring Lake formed when Lock and Dam No. 2 was completed in the 1930s. Unlike many parks that tease you with a vista here, or an overlook there, fully half the trails on Schaar's Bluff overlook the vast sweep of water sprinkled with an archipelago of teardrop shaped islands.

The northern half of the trail winds through an open forest where you can expect the snow to hold on late in the season. To the south you enter an evergreen forest of ponderosa, jack, red and white pines. This northwoods venture leads to a designated overlook with shelter that makes a great spot for a winter picnic.

There is just enough roll to the trails to keep your interest from lagging, but only one real downhill that will intimidate beginners. This park is destined for an even greater future when trails eventually connect Schaar's Bluff with the Archery Trail and over four miles of Mississippi River shoreline. Stay tuned.

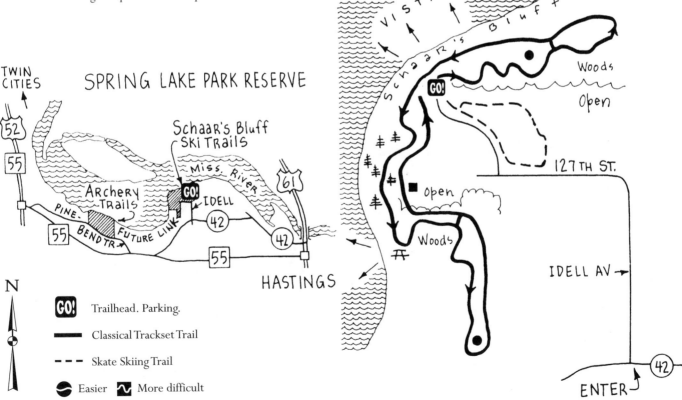

SKI
49
SUNFISH LAKE PARK

Administered by City of Lake Elmo   Phone 777-5510

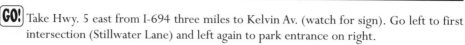

GO! Take Hwy. 5 east from I-694 three miles to Kelvin Av. (watch for sign). Go left to first intersection (Stillwater Lane) and left again to park entrance on right.

Trackset 13.1 km (8.1 mi)   **Skate Ski** No   **Size** 380 acres

Rating All levels, known for its exciting hills.   **Hours** Sunrise to sunset   **Toilet** Outdoors, at entry

Fee Free, MN Ski Pass required   **Sliding Hill** Yes, not packed

---

One of Fred's Best cross country ski areas. Fast, narrow trails through a mature forest.

This is an amazing place to go cross country skiing. It is also a maze of a place to ski at. Folklore has it that these trails began by following deer paths through the woods. The narrow winding trails still give this impression, and though there are signs to help you find your way, the best advice is to keep skiing and know that you won't be lost long.

If you are a beginning skier and a superb navigator, you may be able to follow Ernie's Trail, which is a 3.7 kilometer easier loop. On the flip side, daredevils may wish to give the Powerline "Trail" a whirl when conditions are right. You're skiing at your own risk and if you break a ski – like my buddy Kent – there's no one to blame but yourself.

On weekends this can be a very popular place, but the narrow winding trails provide plenty of intimacy. And with trees so close to the trail the perception of speed on the downhill runs is even greater. There are some near-record-size birch trees and oaks measuring eight feet in diameter in this handsome forest. Amenities may be lacking but the skiing is great.

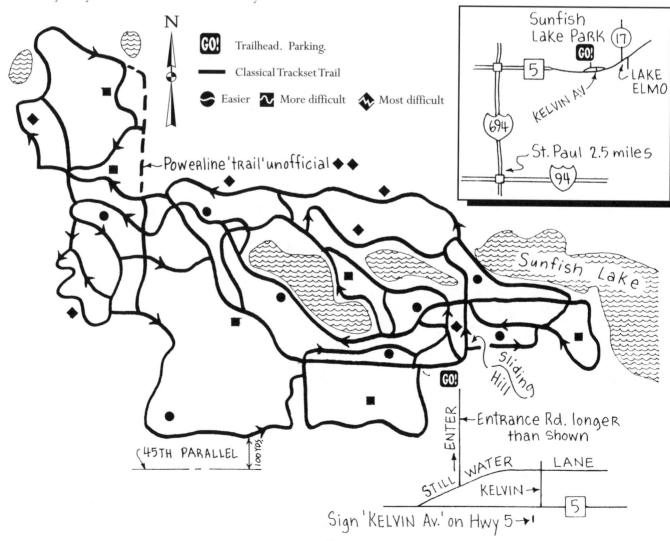

50 WILD RIVER STATE PARK

Administered by Minnesota DNR   Phone 612-583-2125

GO! Take I-35 north and exit at Hwy. 95 in North Branch. Go right (east) 10 miles to Co. Rd. 12 and left (north) on Co. Rd. 12 to park entrance.

Trackset 56 km (35 mi)   **Hours** 8 a.m. to 10 p.m.   **Size** 6,803 acres

Rating Groomed trails for all levels of ability   **Fee** $4 two-day, $20 annual. MN Ski Pass required

Warming House Trail Center open same hours as park with wood stove, fireplace, seating for 70, good food (chili, hot dogs, chocolate), washrooms, water and **no-wax ski rental.**

Interpretive Center Open weekends 10 to 5 (often Wednesday to Friday as well) with naturalist-led programs, displays, a unique weather station, popular bird feeders, washrooms and water.

Snowshoeing Naturalist-led hikes on Saturdays include snowshoes. **Snowshoe rental** also available

Cabins and Camping Popular guest house (sleeps eight with fireplace), camper cabins, drive-in and ski-in sites

A five-star cross country ski center with over 50 kilometers of wilderness trails. Trumpeter swans, eagles and porcupines are among the visitors at this sprawling riverside park.

Wild River State Park is the first place I call when I find out another band of snow has passed just north of the Cities. This is a great place for a day trip and with such an extensive trail system it's no wonder that the camper cabins and guest house are often reserved weeks in advance. The Pine Ridge campsite has a great view and large pines.

The park hugs the nationally designated "wild and scenic" St. Croix River for over 18 miles. Observe the open waters closely at the Nevers Dam Site and the Deer Creek outlet. The huge white birds gliding across as magnificent apparitions are trumpeter swans. These have been regular residents the past three years.

The McElroy Visitor Center overlooks the St. Croix Valley and is a great place to introduce yourself to the natural wonders of the park. A weather station details up-to-the-minute conditions, and the bird feeder attracts a wide range of winter species including purple finches, redpolls, juncos, nuthatches and woodpeckers. A new outdoor exhibit, "Vanished Forest," recreates the experience of walking amidst 200-foot-tall white pines.

The resident naturalist leads popular snowshoe hikes on Saturday afternoons that focus on animal tracking, landscape interpretation and bird identification. Sunday afternoon programs discuss the park's natural history (originally the uplands were largely oak savanna, the lowlands floodplain forest, with the great pineries spreading north from the Sunrise River), human history (Native American homeland, fur post and 1849 military road site), and current landscape restoration efforts.

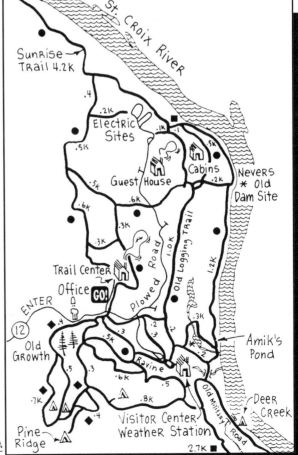

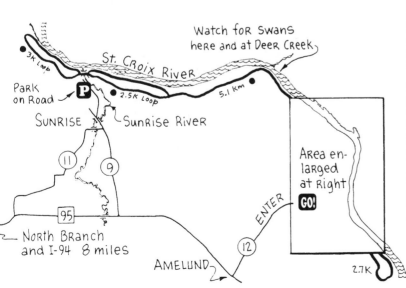

WM. O'BRIEN STATE PARK

SKI 51

Administered by Minnesota DNR   Phone 433-0500

GO! Take the Hwy. 97 exit just north of where I-35E and I-35W join and go right (east) about 13 miles to Hwy. 95. (Note: Hwy. 97 jogs left and right at Hwy. 61.) Turn right (south) and go 1 mile to park entrance on right.

Trackset 19.2 km (12 mi)   **Skate Ski** 16 km (10 mi)   **Size** 1,400 acres

Rating All abilities. Tracks set, not groomed.   **Fee** $4 two-day, $20 annual pass   **Hours** 8 a.m. to 10 p.m.

Warming House Interpretive Center (open 9 to 4) has natural and cultural history exhibits, plus washrooms, water, sodas and seating around a wood-burning stove. **Camping** 6 sites with electricity

An old friend of local cross country skiers, William O'Brien has the terrain, wildlife, creature comforts and camaraderie that are perennial favorites.

William O'Brien State Park is located two miles north of Marine-on-St. Croix where the first saw mill in Minnesota was built in 1839 – a full decade before Minnesota even became a United States territory. The St. Croix River Valley was then forested with magnificent stands of white pine. O'Brien, a logger who grew wealthy on these natural riches, bought river frontage here that was later donated to the state by his daughter, Alice, in 1945. Today, a few remnant old growth pine trees along the river are solitary reminders of the site's former glory.

This is a wonderful place to ski and the vistas of the river valley from high atop the bluffs are unbeatable. There is nearly 300 feet of elevation change within the park and better skiers always gravitate toward the outer loops at the western park perimeter. There is plenty of skiing for those less skilled on the wide plateau that surrounds the park's trailhead at the Interpretive Center.

A speedy traditional trail follows the closed park road down to some easier and quite scenic skiing along the river. Evidence of the park's geologic past can be seen in the 20-ton granite boulder carried down from Duluth by a glacier.

A naturalist leads several winter programs at William O'Brien including winter astronomy, animal tracking and snowshoe hikes (BYO). Watch for wild turkeys in the wooded northwest corner of the park, beaver lodges in the southwest and deer everywhere. Children and old-timers alike are invited to participate in the annual William O'Brien Ski Race that is held the first Sunday in February.

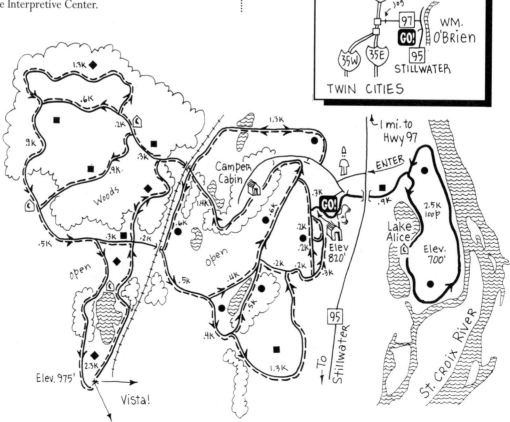

Administered by Wisconsin DNR   Phone 715-386-5931

GO! Take I-94 east into Wisconsin 4 miles and exit at U.S. Hwy. 12. Go north on 12 to County U, turn left and follow signs to park entrance on left.

Trackset 16 km (10 mi)

Rating Well groomed trails for all abilities

Fee Nonresident car – $7 daily, $25 annual

Warming House Nature Center open Friday to Sunday 9 to 4 with displays, portapotty and sodas

Winter Walking 1 km loop

Skate Ski Same length

Size 3,000 acres

Hours 6 a.m. to 11 p.m.

Camping Ski-in campsites plus 6 RV sites

> *W*illow Falls is the scenic highlight of the tour, but this is a pleasant escape into the country for all east metro skiers. It is closer than you think.

Falling water, below freezing temperatures and a bright winter sun create compelling sculptures of ice framed by sandstone walls. Willow River has three combination dam and waterfalls. Willow Falls drops over 100 feet with a staircase of natural rock ledges stepping down below the sheer vertical gates of the dam. A narrow trail leads to the site and is a must-see for all visitors.

I visited the park on New Year's Day and found over 60 cars in the parking lot. Expecting trailside traffic jams, I was happy to realize that the park was big enough for everyone. We saw less than 20 people the entire afternoon. Pine plantations, prairie and a second-growth hardwood forest cover the rolling terrain.

The land's original white homesteader, William Scott, arrived here to stay in 1849. His family gravesite lies on top of a high hill with a commanding view of the Willow River, that once flowed freely through this valley.

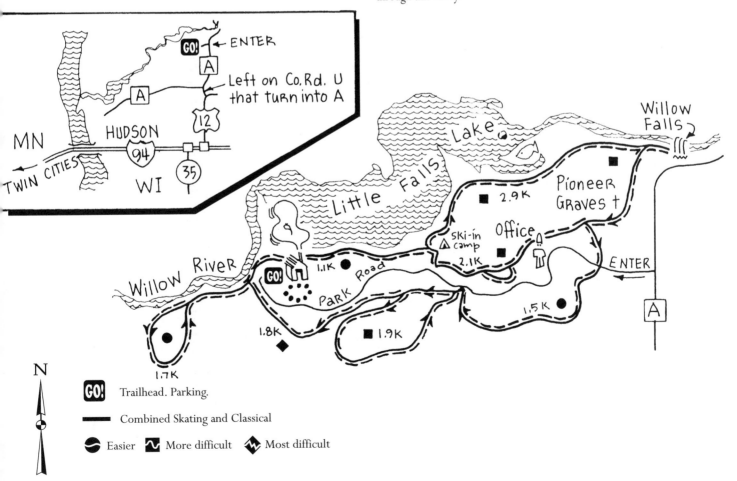

GO! Trailhead. Parking.

—— Combined Skating and Classical

◗ Easier   〰 More difficult   ◈ Most difficult

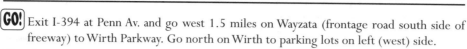

GO! Exit I-394 at Penn Av. and go west 1.5 miles on Wayzata (frontage road south side of freeway) to Wirth Parkway. Go north on Wirth to parking lots on left (west) side.

Trackset 13.2 km (8.2 mi)   **Skate Ski** 4.8 km (3 mi)   **Size** 739 acres

Rating Beginner trails, intermediate (lit) trail, and a nifty expert course near I-394   **Hours** Sunrise to 9 p.m.

Warming House A Swiss Chalet is the center for activities mid-December through mid-February, open Thursday through Sunday until about 9 p.m. Snack food, hot chocolate, washrooms, lessons, **no-wax ski rental** available.

Sliding Hill Right side of Chalet. "The longest ride in town."   **Snowshoeing** Rental available. Stay off the ski trails.

Tubing One area with rope tow and groomed hill. **Snow tube rental** available.

A winter sports mecca in Minneapolis. The drive past Birch Pond after a fresh snowfall will transport you to an alpine state of mind. And if nature doesn't cooperate, Wirth makes its own snow.

Theodore Wirth first toured the park land he would oversee in January 1906 using two horses and a sleigh, crossing what was then open country as he traveled from park to park. Wirth spent the next four decades developing these natural resources into one of the finest municipal park systems in the country. And after he retired the best of the best was named in his honor.

The Swiss Chalet is the perfect headquarters for a winter recreational retreat. Completed in 1923, the hand-crafted building was based on a miniature chalet that Wirth had brought back from his honeymoon in Switzerland years before.

Both a skate skiing course and an intermediate traditional trail start from the chalet. As you ski up and through the forest the park feels wild and remote. Gaining the crest and turning back, the glittering Minneapolis skyscrapers in the afternoon sun may startle you with their closeness. This is also the prettiest place in the Cities for nighttime skiing. The long, fast downhill out onto the golf course should stay etched in your mind. But my favorite adventures at Wirth Park are the labyrinthine wood trails that skirt the tamarack bog near I-394. These narrow, twisting trails are a joy and just minutes from downtown. Tamaracks, denizens of the far north, are at the southern edge of their range in Minneapolis.

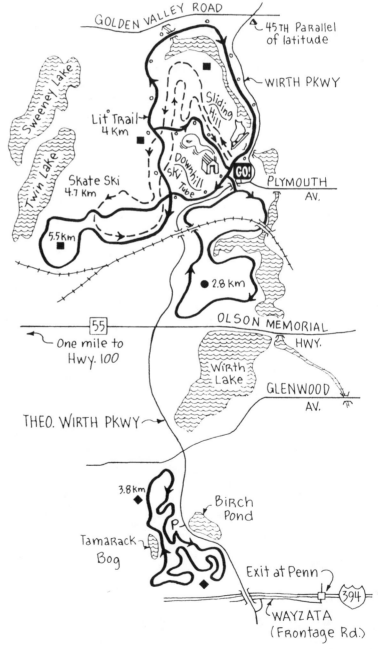

N

GO!   Start of ride. Parking.

———   Classical Trackset Trail

- - - -   Skate Skiing Only

● Easier   ⏦ More difficult   ◆ Most difficult

SKI 54 WOODBURY CITY TRAILS

Administered by City of Woodbury   Phone 731-5788

Fee Free, MN Ski Pass required   **Hours** 6 a.m. to 10 p.m.

Winter Walking Over 35 miles of paved paths are plowed. Phone 731-5788 for map.

> *Ojibway Park is the recreational hub of Woodbury. Thanks to the progressive city policy that requires developers to dedicate land around lakes for trails, there is a great network of paths for winter walking.*

CARVER LAKE PARK

Winter Walking 2 miles   **Size** 138 acres

Carver Lake Park offers a pretty but relatively short romp through a remnant section of hills and woods. Some elderly and distinguished bur oaks can be found on the ridgetop along with some lake views.

The park has a nice secluded feeling marred only by the high-wire easement and the lack of trail signage.

OJIBWAY PARK

Trail 4.8 km (3 mi)   **Size** 121 acres

Rating Mostly easier   **Skating Rink**

Warming House Open 4 to 10 weekdays, Saturday 9 to 10 p.m. and Sunday 11 to 7. Washrooms and water.

A large active park with the longest (albeit least natural) trail system in the city. Trails are groomed for traditional skiing.

TAMARACK NATURE PRESERVE

Trail 3 km (2 mi)   **Size** 178 acres

Rating Easier, no amenities

Don't fret that the evergreens have dropped all their needles. They're supposed to. Tamaracks are deciduous conifers with needle-like leaves that turn a golden yellow before dropping each fall.

The tamarack bog found here is at the southern edge of its natural range and offers some flat skiing through a small, but wild scene.

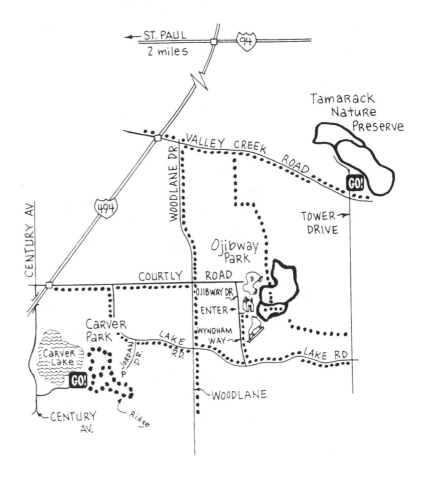

N

GO! Trailhead. Parking.

⸺ Classical Trackset Trail

⊖ Easier   〰 More difficult

•••• Winter Walking

Getting a jump on the season at Buck Hill — November 29, 1995.

DOWNHILL SKIING & SNOWBOARDING

Downhill skiing in Minnesota is for everyone. There are ten ski areas nearby with vertical drops ranging from 40 feet to over 400 feet. This is the Land of Lakes, not the Rocky Mountains, but there is plenty of terrain for all levels of skiers. Jean-Claude Killy may not be home-grown, but Minnesotan Trace Worthington, the most successful men's freestyle skier in the world, has won 37 World Cup titles.

While there are mogul fields to challenge even the best skiers, the local hills have plenty of terrain that will appeal to casual skiers and newcomers. Every ski area offers lessons and affordable learn-to-ski packages. Snowboarding lessons, rentals and special "fun parks" are now featured everywhere as well.

Fickle Minnesota winters are supplemented with state-of-the-art snowmaking and nightly grooming. You can ski from Thanksgiving to Easter, and most local ski areas close their doors in spring for lack of skiers, not lack of snow. Every downhill ski area in this book has 100 percent snowmaking coverage, is 100 percent lit for night skiing and grooms their slopes every single night (or day) to keep icy conditions to a minimum. One memorable February day in 1996, I went skiing 24 hours after rain and sleet turned my lawn brown. The day was sunny, the temperature was in the mid-40s, and snow conditions were excellent on the slopes.

HISTORY

Although cross country skiing dates back some 9,000 years, the telemark binding, which made downhill skiing possible, was not developed until the 1850s in Norway, and for several decades it was used primarily for ski jumping. Alpine, or downhill skiing as we know it today developed after the turn of the century, but didn't really take off until after World War II.

The father of modern downhill skiing was a Minnesotan — for four years anyway. Sondre Norheim was born in 1825 and grew up in the town of Morgedal in the Telemark district of Norway. He left "the single most important mark on sport skiing — the heel binding." For the first time in over 7,000 years of skiing history, a skier was able to turn and stop, or link turns and continue downhill.

"Down a St. Paul Hill"

Telemark turns eliminated the need for these long poles (used to slow a skier's descent). Winter Carnival edition of Northwest Magazine, *1887.*

The binding allowed the distinctive, bent-knee telemark turn that is still practiced by skiers around the globe. Norheim was an extraordinary athlete as well and won several competitions in the 1850s and 1860s in ski jumping and cross country skiing tournaments. Although the new binding opened the way for downhill or slalom (sla-slope, lom-ski tracks) skiing, this alpine form of recreation and competition was still decades away.

When times turned tough in Norway, Sondre Norheim, now past his competitive prime, moved his family in 1884 to the town of Oslo, Minnesota. Two of his brightest ski students moved here as well, and more of their stories can be found in the history sections of the SKI JUMPING and DOWNHILL SKIING chapters.

In 1894, the first ski patents in the world were taken out by Fritz Huitfeldt in Nor-

way. His toe irons still allowed the free heel necessary for skiers to go up hills and mountains but were much more secure and durable than the osier and leather bindings that preceded them. Interestingly, the telemark ski, with its narrow waist, mid-ski camber and flared ends, remained the standard for all types of skiing from the 1850s until the 1930s when shorter, wider downhill skis were developed.

The Northland Ski Company began in St. Paul in 1911.

Hart Ski Manufacturing Company is based in St. Paul. A metal working firm founded in 1942, Hart began making skis in 1955. Their Javelin freestyle ski was called the "Ferrari of skis" when it was introduced in 1966. A Limited Edition Javelin Anniversary model was released in 1996. Another St. Paul firm makes Sled Dogs – downhill snow skates aimed at the estimated 12 million in-line skaters nationwide.

GETTING STARTED

Reliable snowmaking, excellent grooming, affordable prices and not-too-steep hills make the metro area a great place to pick up the sport or revive old skills. It had been nearly 20 years since my college forays out west when I began researching this chapter. I was pleasantly surprised that my body remembered what to do.

Learn-to-ski packages are available at every hill and these often include complimentary lessons or reduced rates on an instructional program. "Ski Wee" series are available for children as young as four years old. Older beginners are catered to as well. A first-time skier in her forties was put at ease when her instructor turned out to be a lady in her 60s.

First-time skiers use slow, extra short skis as they learn how to turn, stop, ride the chairlifts and – most importantly – get up when they fall.

The nation's first chairlift debuted at Gunstock, New Hampshire in 1938, thanks to a federally funded work program developed during the depression. New Hampshire claims two other firsts – the first racing trail, the Taft, cut at Cannon Mountain in 1929, and the first ski school opened at Peckett's-on-Sugar Hill in 1930.

A couple of Brits, Sir Henry Lunn and Frederick Roberts, founded the first Alpine Sports Club in 1903 in Switzerland. Austrian ski pioneer Mathias Zdarsky set up the first slalom course in 1905, and the first club matches were held in 1928 between Arlberg and Kandahar. In 1936, downhill skiing joined cross country skiing and ski jumping in the Winter Olympics.

As skiers were going faster, more legs were being broken. Yet another Norwegian, Hjalmar Hvam, was just awakening from the ether of the operating table in 1939 when he asked for a pencil and paper. Having broken the same leg for the second time on Mt. Hood, Hvam dreamed up the first marketed safety ski release. Although it didn't become popular until after World War II, this new safety binding and the advent of uphill tows, jump-started the alpine ski industry.

Buck Hill claims bragging rights as the oldest local ski area. Their first brochure, released in October 1954, touted four tows and open slopes with a 313-foot vertical drop. In today's ever-expanding metro world it should be noted that Trollhaugen began operations in 1950 with one rope tow and three runs. Wirth Park predates both areas with downhill skiing going back to the 1930s.

Learning to ski at Hyland Hills.

DRESS FOR SUCCESS

Frostbite is forever so don't take chances. Waiting in line and riding the lifts generates little heat, so remember this to stay warm:

1. Never wear cotton next to the skin.

2. Instead, start with a WICKING LAYER of polypropylene (silk or polyolifin) from top to toes.

3. An INSULATING LAYER of polar fleece, synthetic pile or wool is next.

4. Finally, wear a WIND-BLOCK LAYER of Gore-Tex or coated nylon on top.

5. Mittens are in style again, and caps (a poly balaclava topped with a fleece-lined bomber hat is the ultimate) are essential.

SKI INJURY-FREE

Downhill skiing is a relatively safe sport and most injuries can be avoided by following some simple precautions.

- **Ski in control, know how to stop.** Out-of-control skiing is the number one cause of injuries. Even experienced skiers benefit from a refresher lesson.

- **Fall correctly. Don't try to get up while still moving.** When falling, keep arms forward. Keep skis together, keep hands over skis.

- **Don't use pole straps.** Falling while grasping a pole can result in "skiers thumb" – painful and debilitating.

- **Don't ski when you're tired.** That last run really could be. Ski sober.

- **Stay off icy slopes**. Don't follow skiers down the steepest slopes until you are ready.

- **Stay on groomed trails,** watch for other skiers on merging trails and remember that people ahead of you have the right of way.

Courtesy of Hennepin Parks

SNOWBOARDING IS HERE TO STAY

It's your attitude not your aptitude that determines your altitude, Dude.

Hey, here's something your kid (read younger brother, punk next door, etc.) can do and YOU CAN'T! Snowboarding is no longer the next big thing, it's here to stay. Snowboarding is the major growth area in the downhill industry. It's a clearly established sport that now captures from 15% to 25% of the local downhill attendance.

Sure, the majority of boarders are teens who tend to wear bright, baggy clothing and speak in tongues – *He's the sauce, Bone it out! Get Phat!!* But I can tell you from personal experience that boarding is great exercise, has a graceful motion (that I usually achieved just before falling) and is a kick to watch. Local areas are outdoing each other in building new snowparks to give snowboarders the chance to strut their stuff, or toot their stiffies as they say.

Check it out. You can get rentals and lessons almost anywhere. First-timers find snowboarding easier to learn than skiing. The first day out is tough, but once you find that balancing point, you're set. Just pretend you're riding a bike, as Mark, my instructor, put it. Legs bent, back straight, with both hands up in front.

Heck, you can ride a bike, can't you?

DOWNHILL SKI CLUBS

There are 17 or so local downhill ski clubs that schedule trips from Aspen Alps to the Austrian Alps. The **Sitzmark Ski Club** (545-1151) is the largest with 750 members. Most clubs schedule activities all year long that include bowling, biking, canoeing and more. Cross country skiing and downhill racing are part of some clubs' activities.

The **Minnesota Ski Council (MSC)** is an umbrella organization that publishes the annual *MSC Club Roster* of all local clubs in late summer each year, with a profile and featured list of scheduled trips for each. It is available in most downhill ski shops or by mail. To receive the *MSC Club Roster* send $1 (each) to:

MSC Publications Manager
P.O. Box 4063
St. Paul, MN 55104

All MSC Club members receive the bi-monthly *Minnesota Skier* newspaper that carries news from all the clubs plus articles on ski technique, trip reports, upcoming events, etc. Nonmember subscriptions are available for $6 (6 issues), payable to the Minnesota Ski Council and mailed to the address listed above.

The **Courage Alpine Ski Program** teaches adaptive downhill skiing to people with visual impairments or other physical disabilities. One-on-one instruction is provided by trained volunteers. Phone 520-0215 to volunteer or 520-0495 to take part.

SKI

AFTON ALPS

Administered by Afton Alps   Phone 436-5245

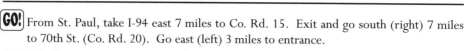

GO! From St. Paul, take I-94 east 7 miles to Co. Rd. 15. Exit and go south (right) 7 miles to 70th St. (Co. Rd. 20). Go east (left) 3 miles to entrance.

Skiable Acres 250   **Scenic Runs** 37   **Vertical Drop** 350 feet

Variety of Terrain Afton has the highest percent of challenging ski runs for the intermediate and better skier.

Lifts 15 double chairs, 3 triple chairs, 2 rope tows, 1 handle-tow   **Hours** Daily 9 am to 10 pm

Snowboarding Half-pipe, rental and complimentary beginner lessons.

Amenities Four chalets with cafeterias (no wait-service) and 3 full bars. Racing program, ski school and **Sled Dogs**.

Afton Alps is the mother of all metro downhill ski areas. A sprawling affair with plenty of terrain for all skiers. It is surrounded on three sides by beautiful Afton State Park.

The sign tells you that all vehicles must use low gear on the steep road down to the main chalets. Right away you get the idea that Afton Alps is a little different from most local downhill ski areas. Evergreens and a steep, wooded hillside paint the backdrop of the Alps Chalet. Walking across the footbridge over Trout Brook to enter the lodge reminded me of one of my favorite Western ski areas. This place has a nice feel to it and I liked the fact you can't see every run from the parking lot. There's room to explore here.

Afton Alps has several challenging runs for better skiers but beginners will enjoy the mellow terrain of the meadows runs and Nancy's

Nursery has what may be the shortest chairlift (100 yards, tops) on the planet. Complimentary lessons are available for beginning skiers and snowboarders who rent equipment and purchase lift tickets.

Afton Alps' proximity to the heart of the Twin Cities means that it gets a lot of use. Fortunately, the 37 runs, four chalets and multiple parking areas ensure easy access and help spread the crowds out. Rugged Afton State Park wraps around the ski area, and telemark skiers (with a State Parks sticker) can enjoy some cross training by hopping onto the park's ski trails at the bottom of the Highlands area.

Expect The Unexpected

Trail and slope conditions vary constantly with weather changes and skier use. Be aware of changing conditions--natural or man-made

Ski Smart.... Ski in Control

Courtesy of Afton Alps

BUCK HILL

Phone 435-7174

GO! Take 35E or 35W south of Burnsville Center and exit at Co. Rd. 46. Turn right (west), then right again on the frontage road to entrance.

Skiable Acres 40   **Scenic Runs** 12   **Vertical Drop** 310 feet

Variety of Terrain Mostly beginner and intermediate   **Hours** Weekdays 10 to 10, Weekends 9 to 10

Lifts (capacity) 3 double chairs, 1 quad chair, 3 rope tows, 1 J-bar and 1 handle-tow for kids

Snowboarding ALJOHNS snowboard park has the only championship groomed half-pipe in the Midwest.

Amenities Restaurant, cafeteria and full bar. Guaranteed learn-to-ski program for skiers and boarders.

One of the best local snowboarding areas has also been named the "legendary capital of American ski racing" by Ski *magazine.*

Buck Hill may be the granddaddy of Twin Cities ski areas, but they know that the kids are the future. First opened in 1954 with a cleared slope, a small building and four rope tows, Buck Hill now offers a state-of-the-art snowboard park that changes through the seasons. Teens love it as they sail over buried cars and slide bars.

If you'd like to "Fly the Buck" or at least give snowboarding a chance, sign up for their *Guaranteed Learn-to-Snowboard* program. Be fore-warned: the first day is the toughest, and you will fall a lot. But once you find your balance point, the learning curve is dramatic. It's easier to pick up from scratch than skiing.

Many of Minnesota's best racers got their start at Buck Hill and some went on to become members of the U.S. Ski Team. Rather amazing considering that there is only one bona fide expert run here.

Today skiers and snowboarders look out onto the I-35 freeway, but in times past they gazed out further. The 1881 *History of Dakota County* explains, "at the west end of Crystal Lake is a high hill, called by the early settlers Buck Hill. From the top of this high eminence the Indians would watch the deer as they came to drink from the cool waters of the lake."

All photos courtesy of Buck Hill

Snowboarders catching some major air at Buck Hill.

S K I

COMO PARK SKI CENTER

Administered by St. Paul Division of Parks and Recreation   See map on page 40.
Phone 488-9673 or 266-6400

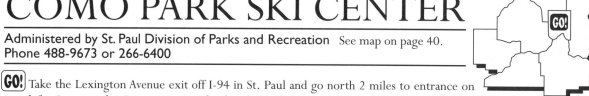

GO! Take the Lexington Avenue exit off I-94 in St. Paul and go north 2 miles to entrance on left. (Just past the Conservatory and Lakeside Pavilion.)

Skiable Acres 5 or so   **Scenic Runs** 2   **Vertical Drop** 70 feet

Variety of Terrain Easy and easier   **Lifts** 2 rope tows

Hours Weekdays 3 to 9 p.m., Sat. 9 to 6 p.m. and Sun. 11 to 6 p.m.

Snowboarding Both runs are open to boarders. Limited rental. Lessons by appointment.

Amenities Chalet with food service, accessory shop, lessons and equipment rental

A full-service, in-town ski area that is about the least intimidating learn-to-ski center around. Cheap!

Downhill skiing is an exciting, lifelong activity that almost anyone can learn. Whether you're four or forty and you want to feel the wind whistling by as you speed down a snowy slope, Como is for you.

Six-lesson learn-to-ski packages will have you ready and raring for the more challenging slopes at Afton Alps or even the Rocky Mountains. Costs are extremely affordable for children and adults (in 1996 they were $40 for students who have their own equipment or $60 including rental and lift tickets).

Como also has groomed trails for cross country skiing and is the perfect place to learn the age-old sport of telemarking. Instructors teach graceful, freeheel turns on special cross country skis that you can use to negotiate terrain from alpine areas to the back country.

Easy and easier downhill skiing at Como Park.

Photo and drawings courtesy of St. Paul Parks and Recreation

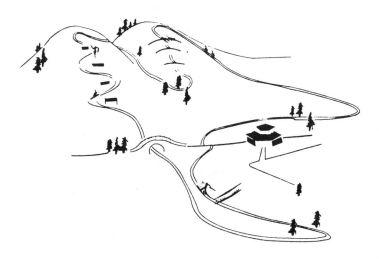

HYLAND HILLS

Administered by Hennepin Parks   Phone 835-4250   See map on page 52.

GO! Exit I-494 at Hwy. 100 (Normandale Blvd.) and go south on Normandale to 84th St. Turn right (west) and go 1/2 mile to Chalet Road. Turn left and go two blocks to entrance.

Skiable Acres 35   **Scenic Runs** 14   **Vertical Drop** 175 feet

Variety of Terrain 60% of the runs are rated beginner, 20% intermediate and 20% expert

Lifts 3 triple chairs, 3 rope tows   **Hours** 10 to 9 weekdays, till 10 p.m. on Friday and Saturday

Snowboarding 100% open with expanded Fun Park featuring all the bells and whistles. Rental and lessons.

Amenities Chalet sports new addition with expanded menu and cafeteria islands. No alcohol and no smoking.

Snowboard central! Catch some air on all the latest pipes, spines and slides, plus the Midwest's largest ski school.

"The Midwest's first and best amateur snowboarding program," is how the brochure reads, and on the day I visited over half the young visitors were snowboarders. Great man-made thrusts of snow have been shaped into a rollicking playground for catching air. Even if you don't board it's almost worth the price of admission just to watch the action under the lifts. The "yard sales" (wipeouts) can be spectacular. If somebody yells out, "Backside fakie mondo," look for someone riding backwards up a halfpipe wall and doing a handspring as they shoot over the top of the lip.

To help newcomers avoid yard sales, Hyland Hills has a wide variety of learn-to-ski programs for children and adults. Downhill skiing and snowboarding, plus the art of telemarking and ski racing, are all taught here. Hyland Hills is one of the gentler ski areas around.

In 1996, Hyland became the first ski area in the U.S. to be entirely nonsmoking — indoors and out.

Photo and drawing courtesy of Hennepin Parks

Thousands of Twin Cities youngsters get their first downhill skiing lessons at Hyland Hills.

MOUNT FRONTENAC

Toll-free phone 1-800-488-5826 or 612-388-5826

GO! One hour south of the Twin Cities. Take Hwy. 61 nine miles south of Red Wing to Ski Road Trail and turn right. Watch for blue signs. The turn is just past where the ski area becomes visible from road.

Skiable Acres 100 (330 total)   **Scenic Runs** 11   **Vertical Drop** 420 feet

Variety of Terrain Take it from the top, with either the Easy Mile or the mogul madness of Baldy

Lifts (capacity) 3 double chairs, 2 rope tows (3,000/hour)   **Hours** Wed. to Fri. 4 to 10, Sat. 9 to 10, Sun. 10 to 8

Snowboarding All runs open to boarders, plus snowpark, lessons and rental equipment

Amenities Restaurant, bar and snack food. Video games, ski school and racing program

> *Set on a steep, wooded Mississippi River bluff with a view, Mount Frontenac features the greatest vertical drop in the metro area.*

Mount Frontenac owns a corner of the beautiful Mississippi River Valley. Their brochure headline advertises this as *A Challenging Experience,* and the steep mogul field of the Baldy run is the toughest in this book. It is clearly the big draw for many visitors and a great warm-up for anyone heading to the Rockies.

Beginners will not feel left out, as the Easy Mile is long enough to simulate a real mountain run. There are very inexpensive learn-to-ski packages as well. The new snowpark lets you ski or board through the trees — another unique feature of this park that makes it worth the drive.

The comfortable glass and wood chalet is nothing fancy, but it has a good variety of soups, Dave's pizza, and even mini corn dogs. A separate adult chalet offers a full bar.

Photo and brochure courtesy of Mount Frontenac

POWDER RIDGE

Toll-free 1-800-348-7734   Local and St. Cloud 398-7200

GO! One hour west of the Twin Cities. Take I-94 west to Hwy. 15 exit. Go left (south) on 15 eleven miles to entrance.

Skiable Acres 70   **Scenic Runs** 15   **Vertical Drop** 290 feet

Variety of Terrain All levels of difficulty   **Lifts** 2 double chairs, 1 quad, 2 rope tows, 2 J-bars

Hours Mon., Wed., Thurs., Fri. 10 to 10, Saturday and holidays 9 to 10, Sunday 9 to 9, Tuesday 4 to 10

Snowboarding 100 % open to boarders, half-pipe, lessons and rental

Amenities Expanded chalet with cafeteria, kids recreation room, adult lounge, ski school

Rising high above the surrounding fields, Powder Ridge is a valuable recreational resource for the west metro area.

Powder Ridge rises like a mirage from the windswept tundra that surrounds it. Like a modern Mayan temple built for the winter gods, Powder Ridge is a glacial phenomena that has been built up even higher to appease the downhill desires of the surrounding populace.

This is small-town skiing at its friendliest. Management goes out of its way to provide a variety of family events, races and special rates designed to attract the frugal skier. Ladies' Thursdays (lunch and lift ticket for twelve dollars), Nine Buck Nights (may be ten by now) and March Madness ("the rates go down as the temperature goes up!") are among the favorites. New Year's Eve Family Ski Night features fireworks and a torchlight parade is a highlight.

I'm easily amused and had a swell time skiing here, watching the sunset and imagining I could see all the way to South Dakota. The half-pipe is right under a lift for your viewing pleasure, and there are just enough runs to keep you from getting bored for a few hours.

Photos courtesy of Powder Ridge

G TROLLHAUGEN, WISCONSIN

GO!

Twin Cities toll-free phone is 433-5141

GO! Go north on 35W or 35E to Hwy. 97 exit. Turn right (east) and go 13 miles to Hwy. 95. Turn left (north) on 95 and go 6 miles to Hwy. 243. Go right (east) across the St. Croix River to Wisconsin Hwy. 35 and turn left (north) 3 miles to Dresser and then right (east) on Co. Rd. F 1 mile to entrance.

Skiable Acres 80   **Scenic Runs** 22   **Vertical Drop** 280 feet

Variety of Terrain About 70% intermediate and advanced with the rest easier skiing

Lifts (capacity) 2 quad chairs, 1 double chair, 7 rope tows (10,000/hour)

Hours Open until midnight weekends, 10 pm weekdays

Snowboarding 100% open plus snowpark with quarter pipes, spine, tabletops and sliderail. Rental and lessons

Amenities Full service restaurant with 16-foot salad bar, private on-slope picnic sites and game arcade

Family fun on the slopes and plenty of apres ski options inside. Midnight skiing on weekends and a unique snowpark for snowboarders.

Trollhaugen is a little farther away, less crowded on weekends and family oriented. The half-pipe has been replaced with an exciting new snowpark that features the latest attractions for boarders. The spine — an artificially formed ridge — can be attacked from either side and is sure to be popular.

Skiers enjoy the fast action on Storebakken, the Chute and Jumping Judy, but what sets the Troll apart from other local areas is Haug Wild and, especially, the Fall Line. These two runs drop sharply off the side of a man-made butte. Although short, they're among the steepest drops in the metro area. I ran at least half of Haug Wild on my back. Regrettably, these two runs are currently served only by a rope tow.

Apres ski action is notable. There is a game arcade for the kids, adult lounge and full restaurant serving everything from burgers to lobster. Banquet and catering services are offered year-round. Trollhaugen began its operation in 1950 with 3 runs and a rope tow.

Courtesy of Trollhaugen

WELCH VILLAGE

Twin Cities toll-free phone 222-7079 See page 36.

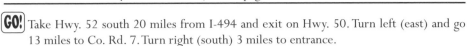

GO! Take Hwy. 52 south 20 miles from I-494 and exit on Hwy. 50. Turn left (east) and go
13 miles to Co. Rd. 7. Turn right (south) 3 miles to entrance.

Skiable Acres 135   **Scenic Runs** 36   **Vertical Drop** 350 feet

Variety of Terrain Equal parts beginner to expert   **Hours** Daily 9 a.m. to 10 p.m.

Lifts (capacity) 5 double chairs, 1 triple, 2 quad, 1 handle-tow for children (10,500/hour)

Snowboarding Snowpark for boarders with variety of jumps, lessons and rental equipment

Amenities Ski tune-up service, lodging for groups of 25 or more, restaurant, full bar, weekend barbeques

> *Nestled in the New England-like Cannon Valley, Welch Village is a large area with a good variety of intimate runs carved out of the wooded ravines.*

A handsome, airy ski chalet and some of the most challenging local runs make Welch Village a winner. This is a charming area to ski and although it is one of the larger metro ski areas, it has a reputation as an undiscovered gem.

There are some full-tilt mogul fields to knock your dentures loose, but there are also plenty of runs for beginners. They even have a new handle-tow for youngsters. Families or groups with cross country skiers can split up and enjoy skate skiing or traditional skiing on the adjacent Cannon Valley Trail.

Welch Village is always trying something new. They were one of the first areas to feature Snow Dogs, and in 1996–97 they will have an adventure center for parabolic skiers. These shorter skis feature fat tips and radical sidecuts for carving turns like you've never seen.

Madd Jaxx Barbeque takes place outdoors on the east end every Saturday and Sunday. The mountain cabins are available for groups that want to spend the night.

Graphics courtesy of Welch Village

SKI 1

WILD MOUNTAIN

Twin Cities toll-free phone 257-3550 (or 1-800-447-4958) Local phone 465-6315

GO! Take 35E or 35W north to Hwy. 8 exit and turn right. Go east to Taylors Falls and then left (north) on Co. Rd. 16 seven miles to entrance.

Skiable Acres 100   **Scenic Runs** 23   **Vertical Drop** 300 feet

Variety of Terrain Neatly divided in thirds for beginner, intermediate and expert skiers

Lifts (capacity) Four quads (11,000/hour)   **Hours** 100% lit till 10 pm (9 pm Sunday and 3 am late Friday)

Snowboarding All runs open to boarders, rental and lessons available. Terrain garden open to skiers and boarders.

Amenities Cafeteria and bar plus 2 reservable on-hill decks. Ski lessons. Banquet room(s) available.

A scenic area overlooking the St. Croix River, Wild Mountain prides itself on the best groomed runs around.

Only an hour — and a relaxed world away — from the Cities, Wild Mountain grooms its trails every night so you can arrive to a "white carpet" every morning. Two-thirds of the area is for beginners and intermediate-level skiers but *You Asked For It* is a great mogul run.

Wild Mountain is set in a nice hardwood forest with no development in sight. There are a few conifers mixed in to preserve the memory of the grand pine forest that once filled the St. Croix Valley. This is probably one of the quieter downhill areas around due to its more remote locale. Do not be surprised, though, if a few school buses pull up midweek. They help support the operation.

The ski chalet has a pleasant ambiance enhanced by historic photos of nearby Taylors Falls, handsome old snowshoes and antique wooden skis decorating the walls. There is a great old pennant declaring the area a winter wonderland, and after a fresh snowfall I'm sure you'll agree.

WIRTH PARK

Administered by Minneapolis Park and Recreation Board   Phone 522-4584

GO! Exit I-394 at Penn Avenue and go west 1.5 miles on Wayzata (frontage road on south side of freeway) to Wirth Parkway. Go north on Wirth to entrance at Plymouth Av.

Scenic Runs 1

Vertical Drop 40 feet

Variety of Terrain Easy as pie

Lifts 1 rope tow

Hours Mid-December to mid-February, Thursday and Friday 5 to 9 pm, Saturday 9 to 9 and Sunday noon to 8 pm

Snowboarding Rental and lessons

Tubing Rental and big hill

Amenities Chalet with snack food and children's rental equipment. Saturday lessons.

The world's smallest downhill ski facility. Great starter course for kids and people who are afraid of heights.

Nostalgia, convenience and low costs are the attraction at Wirth Park. Boomers who remember their own first stabs at downhill skiing now bring their children here to get them started on their way to Vail — or at least Hyland Hills.

The Swiss-style chalet set amidst the surrounding pines lends an authentic atmosphere to winter sports at Wirth. Cross country skiing, sledding and skating can also be enjoyed. The biggest hill here is reserved for tubing. Tube rental is available at the chalet.

Courtesy of Minneapolis Parks Board

The first downhill ski clinics were held at Wirth Park in the late 1930s. This photo by Walter Dahlberg is from 1940.

ICE CLIMBING

After you've done it all, there is still ice climbing.

Ice climbing as a sport began in Scotland in the 1940s but has only been available locally for the last couple of years. There are only a few spots in the country where you can sample this exciting adventure and one of them is in St. Paul. The unique geology of Lilydale Park produces 30-to-40-foot-high ice falls along the bluff.

Unlike waterfalls on a river, these ice falls form each winter where water seeps out of the blufftop and freezes.

The sport is reasonably safe and surprisingly accessible – I first read about ice climbing in an article in *Silent Sports* magazine that was written by a first-time climber about to turn 70.

Climbing at Lilydale Park requires a permit from the city and specialized skills – plus equipment you probably don't have lying around in the basement.

The folks at Vertical Endeavors on St. Paul's East Side can provide you with all of the equipment, training and permits you'll need for about $100 (for a one day excursion).

My day on ice began at their indoor climbing facility off Arcade Avenue. Todd Peterson, our guide, set Sandy and me up with our equipment and talked with us a little about the sport. It is very similar to rock climbing but ecologically superior since climbing bolts are not used and all other evidence of the climbs melt away in the spring.

The first thing you notice is how sharp everything is. The ice axes are evil-looking, with a long serrated blade on top and short, sharpened points at the bottom of the handles. There are insulated plastic boots onto which you strap a 12-prong crampon. The business end of these crampons have two, one-inch-long sharpened steel points sticking straight out from the toes. Think of the boots as seriously-spiked golf shoes.

Now that we have properly-sized equipment, we place it carefully in the trunk and drive out through Harriet Island's riverfront to Lilydale Park. The ice falls are just visible on the bluffs when you park and look across Pickerel Lake, about a 20 minute walk away. Following the curve of the bluff, the falls form a natural amphitheater with curtains of shimmering ice – almost blue early in the season when they are first forming and more of a soft yellow later in the year.

Ice climbing guide, Todd Peterson, holds the rope attached to Sandy's safety harness.

Ice climber on one of the many climbing routes at Lilydale Park.

Fred's Photos, 1995

But the beauty of the ice falls aren't uppermost on my mind as we wait for Todd to set up ropes on the top of the bluff. Ice climbing, like rock climbing, is a two-person operation. While one person climbs, another watches from below with control over the rope onto which the climber is attached. The block-and-tackle arrangement on top works like a pulley so that when – not if – a climber slips or falls they will only slide a few feet before the rope catches them.

The theory of climbing is simple. You kick the pointed toe spikes into the ice while reaching above and hammering the axes into the wall of ice above. It is much like climbing a ladder, and it is pretty amazing that the one-inch toe spikes will easily support your weight.

It is a bright March day with the temperature beginning its slow climb into the low 40s as we get underway. The warmer temperature means the ice is softer and easier to penetrate with our climbing tools.

The crampons provide good footing as I walk up the slanted apron of ice below the falls. Roped up and wielding a steel ice axe in each hand, I'm ready to either climb a wall of ice or take on the toughest derelict who's ever hung out in this still underdeveloped park.

We spend the day trying different routes up the falls. Unless you are a carpenter by trade, the arms are the first to tire. Even with the softer ice it can take several swings with the ice axe to set a grip.

My only mishap occurs later in the day as I start to get weary. Jamming the toe spikes into the ice wall, I slip just a bit and spikes on my right foot slice through my left pant leg, pinning it to the ice. Had I slipped another inch to the left, I would have shish-kabbobed my calf muscle. Instead, no harm is done except for ruining a favorite pair of winter pants. If you are looking to get an edge up on winter, here's your chance.

GETTING STARTED

There are many climbing schools in town, but as of this writing, only Vertical Endeavors has climbing equipment (it can be rented or purchased) and an experienced guide service. All of their guides are American Mountain Guide Service members with extensive training. They also have a rock gym open year-round.

Vertical Endeavors

Business Office/Mailing Address	Rock Gym
519 Payne Avenue	open daily
St. Paul, MN 55101	St. Paul, MN
Phone 774-9327	776-1430

ICE CLIMBING EVENTS

The ice climbing capitol of North America is located up the North Shore in Thunder Bay, Ontario, Canada, where Shaun Parent runs North of Superior Climbing Company (phone 807-344-9636).

Besides offering guide services and lessons, Parent coordinates the annual **Ice Fest** in mid-March. This event draws climbers from as far away as Seattle and Tokyo. There are over 100 waterfalls — up to 328-feet-high around Thunder Bay.

Fred on ice.

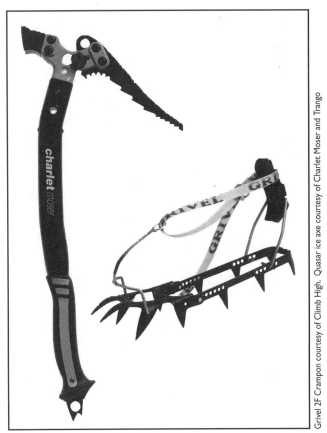

Close-up of an ice axe and crampons.

Grivel 2F Crampon courtesy of Climb High. Quasar ice axe courtesy of Charlet Moser and Trango

Two-year-old Steven Tatro ponders the significance of catching his first fish on Wirth Lake in 1957.

ICE FISHING

*U*p *north they meet the demon head-on. They walk right out to the center of a lake, build a shack the
size of a refrigerator, cut a hole in the ice, fish and drink beer.*

Jeff Cesario
"Winter sports for the semi-broke"
City Pages, Winterlude, 1982-83

When I was just a bit older than the tyke on the left, I caught my first, and last, perch ice fishing. Although ice fishing is not an aerobic sport, it is a long-standing Minnesota tradition. Children are especially vulnerable to ice accidents, so take care. Phone the **Minnesota Department of Natural Resources**, Boat and Water Safety Section at 296-3310 for current regulations and safety tips. Good Luck!

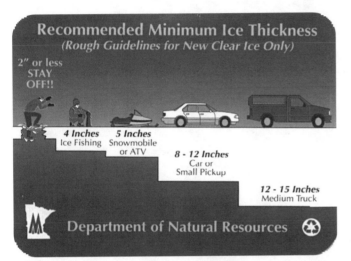

Ice fishing is more of a social phenomena than a sport. It's an excuse to get outdoors, visit with a few buddies and have some laughs. If you catch a fish, hey, so much the better. If your cronies are not tuned into this "action," you can call the **Minnesota Department of Tourism** at 296-5029 to receive a free copy of their *Ice Fishing* brochure. This pamphlet has a statewide listing of resorts and shops where you can rent or purchase everything you'll need, from a portable fish house to a power ice auger.

Small communities of ice fishing huts pop up on most every lake in the metro area when the ice gets thick enough. (See chart at left.) Drive out to one of these, knock on the door and be amazed at the level of comfort and convenience these compact shelters afford — VCRs, stereos and chemical toilets are common. To truly appreciate this Minnesota madness you must head north. Good-sized towns form on the ice of Mille Lacs Lake, complete with plowed roads and self-appointed mayors. And the true believers go one step further. The **International Eelpout Festival** has been held in mid-February on Leech Lake every year since 1980. Phone 800-833-1118 to find out how you can join the revelry.

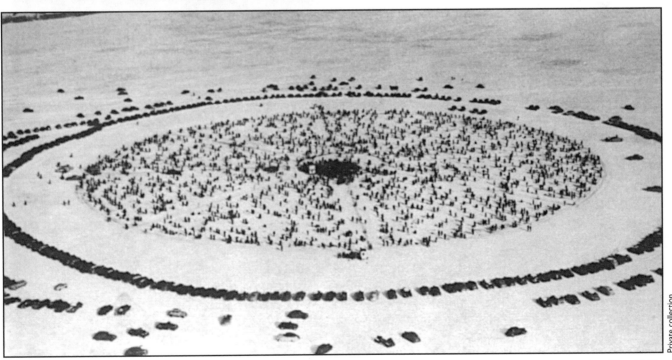

Aerial photo of the first "World's Original Ice Fishing Contest" in 1947 on White Bear Lake. From the St. Paul Winter Carnival Booklet, 1961.

Skaters enjoying "North America's largest outdoor refrigerated skating rink" at the John Rose Minnesota Oval.

ICE SKATING

The pale, cold moon streamed down on the ice,
And painted many a quaint device
of tree and shrub, and forms so fair,
That flitted along like spirits of air.

And the glittering ice a mirror seemed,
While the skaters wandered, as if they dreamed,
Hither and thither, like rays of light,
Or angelic stars in the quiet night.

But one was fairer than all to me;
And I gazed in a gloaming of ecstacy
As she fluttered, twirled, and sped along,
While a ripple of love was my beautiful song.

And the harp of my heart with her step kept time,
While her motion itself was a Runic Rhyme;
And her silv'ry laugh as she sped away
Attuned my harp to a rapturous lay.

Ah Natalie Cherie! when hand in hand
We skated among that happy band,
You little thought that among them all
'twas you alone that had me in thrall!

Cherie Natalie by "Marcie"
from *The Skater's Text-Book* 1868

Heaven knows we'll never walk on water – but in the Twin Cities we can skate on it.

Ice skating picks up each year where in-line skating leaves off. It's great exercise, fun with friends and there are a wealth of local places to enjoy it.

Every municipality in the metro area has places to skate. Call your local parks and recreation department for the nearest neighborhood rink. See "Oh, The Places You'll Go!" below for more information.

Lake of the Isles in Minneapolis and **Lake Como** in St. Paul continue their long tradition of providing some of the most picturesque skating in the region. The **John Rose Minnesota Oval** in Roseville boasts the largest refrigerated outdoor skating rink in North America. This brings to mind the days, nearly a century ago, of the legendary **Hippodrome**. Dubbed "Lake Superior under a roof," this majestic arena on the Minnesota State Fairgrounds was the cradle of the Ice Follies — not to mention many a romance — until World War II ended its reign.

Olympic figure skater Ann Munkholm at Loring Park circa 1924.

Ice skating is most often enjoyed as pure recreation by folks of all ages. Those with a competitive bent should see the "Ice Skating Organizations" section for local speedskating and figure skating clubs. And while the popularity of hockey is no surprise, the Twin Cities is also a hotbed for the European sport of bandy. It's an earlier (1870) version of hockey (without the fights) played on a soccer-sized sheet of ice, using a ball instead of a puck. The Oval has been the site of several international bandy competitions.

The Hippodrome Ice Rink, circa 1915.

HISTORY OF ICE SKATING

The first skates were made with deer bones. The foot-long bones had holes at the ends and leather thongs bound them to the feet. The earliest known bone skates, dating back some 4,000 years, were found in a lake bottom in Switzerland.

About 200 A.D., iron blades set in a wooden plate began to be used in Scandinavia. The first "modern" iron skates, with the blade slotted into the sole of a wooden clog, appeared in Holland in the 1300s. This allowed the "Dutch Roll" skating technique, still used, of pushing off diagonally with one skate while gliding forward on the other.

America's E.V. Bushnell came up with the next innovation in the mid-1800s. His all-metal skate could be clamped, instead of strapped, directly to the shoe or boot. This rigid connection allowed skaters to twist, turn and leap as never before. Figure skating was born, and by 1864 U.S. ballet master Jackson Haynes adapted dance movements to skating and embarked on a triumphant tour of Europe.

The earliest mention of skating in Minnesota that I have found is (oddly enough) from Peg Meier's book, *Too Hot, Went to Lake*. She quotes the diary of Thomas

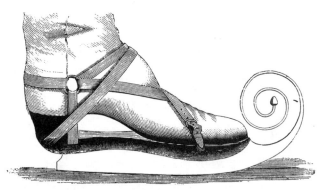

Old-fashioned "turn-over" skate

Scantlebury who lived Sibley County. On November 8, 1856, he writes, "The lake is now crossable for foot passengers, and it has been crossed. It is splendid skating."

Frank O'Brien reminisces in his book *Minnesota Pioneer Sketches* about skating on the Mississippi River.

"There was one winter in particular that was overflowing with enjoyment — the winter of 1860–61. The favorite place for skating was on the river, from the [Hennepin Avenue] suspension bridge, up the river and around Nicollet Island to the east side channel. The skates we used to wear were called "turn-overs" and "stub-toes," grooved runners with heelcorks and straps that were secured so tightly upon the feet that circulation of the blood in those parts was next to impossible.

Quite frequently during the winter we would have the brass band on the ice to discourse music for the many beautiful waltzes. When the snow would cover up the skating grounds, a committee made up from the boys of St. Anthony would set to work and have it shoveled off, thus giving us a pleasure resort unequalled in the western country."

Ice skating at Van Cleve Park in Minneapolis, 1901.

John Strauss Jr. and Sr. at their St. Paul skate shop in 1939. Strauss skates have been used by some of the fastest (dozens of world champions) and most famous (Sonja Henie) skaters in the world.

The popularity of skating continued to climb through the 1890s. Neighborhood rinks opened up throughout St. Paul and Minneapolis. Local firms began making skates. John Strauss Sr. opened in 1887 as a bicycle shop but began making speed, hockey and figure skates under the name Strauss Skate Shop. They are still in business 110 years later in Maplewood.

John S. Johnson became the first local hero when he set world speed-skating records in the 1890s. A long-time Minneapolis resident, he was also a world champion cyclist.

In 1909, two state fair concessionaires, Ed Dickinson and Gale Brooke, opened the Hippodrome Amphitheater to indoor skating (they left the doors open for the ice to freeze). For the next three decades it was the Hipp place to be. St. Paul natives Eddie and Roy Shipstad and Oscar Johnson got their start there. The comedy and figure skating routines they developed blossomed into the *Ice Follies*. In November of 1936, they put 28 Minnesota skaters on a bus and headed for their first engagement in Tulsa, Oklahoma. Another professional ice show, *Holiday on Ice*, also began in Minneapolis.

From the 1930s through the 1950s, the Twin Cities were the hub of speedskating in America. Over 30,000 spectators gathered at Powderhorn Park on January 21, 1934, to watch the U.S. Outdoor Speedskating Championships. Two of the oldest and most distinguished speedskating clubs in the country formed during this era. The Powderhorn Speedskating Club began in 1930. Over the years it has produced several Olympians plus national and world champions including Ken Bartholemew and Bobby Fitzgerald, who shared an Olympic silver medal in 1948. Similar successes were earned by the Midway Speedskating Club that began on Lake Como in 1946.

During the 1950s, Powderhorn racer Johnny Werket became the first American skater to win the International King's Cup Championship at Oslo, Norway. He was World Champion in the 1,500 meter competition five straight years. Minnesotans also made their mark in hockey. Nine Minnesotans were on the U.S. Olympic hockey team that won the gold medal in 1960. Minnesotans, including Coach Herb Brooks, were instrumental in the 1980 Olympic gold medal victory over Russia as well.

Ice Follies originators Eddie Shipstad (aloft) and Oscar Johnson.

The popularity of figure skating for recreation and competition has never waned. Former Minnesotan Jill Trenary won the Women's U.S. Figure Skating Championship in 1990. Skating's popularity as a spectator sport is also strong. Over 10,000 spectators saw the infamous Tonya Harding complete the first American (second woman ever) triple axel jump at the Target Center in 1991.

A new heyday for Minnesota skating may be in the making with the opening of the John Rose Minnesota Oval on December 19, 1993. This world-class facility has already attracted several international speedskating and bandy competitions.

Gerry Scott, winner of her first senior women's title, Ken Bartholemew, (center, with wool racing cap) and Bob Dokken watch the action at Powderhorn Park, 1947.

Courtesy of Minneapolis Parks Board and *Star Tribune*

GETTING STARTED

Get a pair of skates that fit and use the tips in the "Dress for Success" section of the WELCOME TO WINTER chapter to stay warm.

Call your local ice arena or parks and recreation department (phone numbers below) for skating lessons. Contact the clubs listed below for developing your speedskating and figure skating skills.

ICE SKATING ORGANIZATIONS AND EVENTS

There is no shortage of groups that you can get involved with if you are interested in figure skating, ice dancing, speedskating or bandy. Presidents of individual clubs change yearly, so contact the associations listed below to find out which club meets your needs.

Twin City Figure Skating Association

Merry Fragomeni, President   Phone 332-4497
Sylvia Olson, Secretary   Phone 934-4963
Local affiliates of the United States Figure Skating Association (USFSA). There are 14 local clubs with about 1,200 members total. Individual clubs sponsor classes, competitions and USFSA testing programs. Several international competitors live in the Twin Cities.

One newcomer on the block is the **Starlight Ice Dance Club of the Twin Cities** (531-0562). They formed to meet the needs of adult beginning recreational ice dancers and host weekly, social ice dance sessions, group lessons and a **Mid-Winter Mardi Gras** at the Parade Ice Garden in Minneapolis. Join the fun or watch as costumed, choreographed skaters entertain and amuse.

Greater Minnesota Speedskating Association

Phone 646-7058
There are four affiliated clubs in the Twin Cities and Duluth.

John Rose Minnesota Oval

Roseville Parks and Recreation
2800 Arona Street
Roseville, MN 55113
Phone 415-2160
A world-class facility with both indoor and outdoor skating rinks — a 400-meter speedskating track, regulation size bandy rink, hockey rinks and figure skating area. Open to the public for recreational skating and instruction as well.

Midway Speedskating Club

Phone 628-0088, 427-3620 or 633-6007
This group has placed skaters on nine of the past ten U.S. Olympic teams and is hitting its stride at age 50. Youth are encouraged to join, and the action has shifted from Lake Como to the Oval.

Powderhorn Speedskating Club

Phone 827-6373
Although the glory days are gone, there is still some special skating to be had. Powderhorn Lake's "black ice" is harder (when the weather cooperates) than artificial ice and members say it is faster. The Powderhorn Club coaches novices on weekday evenings. Call ahead.

The **St. Paul Winter Carnival** (phone 223-4700) begins at the end of January each year and often includes skating events and competitions. A special ice rink, open to the public, is usually created in a downtown park.

Women's speedskating race at Lake Como during the 1936 St. Paul Winter Carnival.

Minnesota Historical Society Collections

Ice skating at Lake of the Isles is always a treat.

OH, THE PLACES YOU'LL GO!

The Twin Cities sport a dazzling array of outdoor (and indoor) recreational skating rinks, from the intimate urbane setting of **Peavey Plaza** (673-5720) to the wide open spaces of **Lake Minnetonka**. Backyard rinks and local lakes abound. And about once every five or ten years an early freeze, a lack of snow and perhaps a glaze of rain combine so that you can skate *anywhere*. Fred's Best Outdoor Skating Rinks include the following:

• **Centennial Lakes Park**

7499 France Avenue South

Edina, phone 893-9890

Sure, it's in the suburbs, but so is most everybody else. Ten acres of ice, lots of food, fireplaces plus ice skate and kick-sled rentals.

• **Lake Como**

1399 Lexington Parkway North

St. Paul, phone 266-6400 or 488-4920

This rink opens later than many rinks, so call first. A historic site for both competitive and recreational skating. The rebuilt Lakeside Pavilion offers a good selection of concessions.

• **Lake of the Isles**

2500 East Lake of the Isles Parkway

Minneapolis, phone 370-4900

The Currier and Ives setting, well-maintained ice and half-mile island loop make this the most popular skating rink in the city. The trailer and lack of concessions are a small trade-off.

• **Loring Park**

Hennepin Avenue and Harmon Place

Minneapolis, phone 370-4900

Go for the history – world champs like John S. Johnson and Norval Baptie skated here. Go for the setting – the Minneapolis skyline rises above you. Or go for the great après skate, dining and drinks at the Loring Bar.

City Parks and Recreation Phone Numbers (Ice Arenas)

These cities each have a variety of rinks, warming houses and skate rental. Many of the indoor ice arenas offer lessons.

1. Apple Valley (Sports Facility 431-8866) 953-2300
2. Blaine...785-6164
3. Bloomington (Ice Garden 948-8842).....................948-8877
4. Brooklyn Center 569-3400
5. Brooklyn Park (Community Center) 493-8333

6. Burnsville (Ice Center 895-4651) 895-4500
7. Coon Rapids (Cook Ice Arena 421-5035)................767-6462
8. Eagan (Civic Arena 686-1100) 681-4660
9. Eden Prairie (Community Center 949-8470)...........949-8442
10. Edina (Braemar Arena 941-1322) 927-8861

11. Fridley (Columbia Ice Arena 571-6701) 572-3570
12. Inver Grove Heights 450-2585
13. Lakeville (Ames Ice Arena 469-1248) 985-4600
14. Maple Grove (Communty Center)........................494-6200
15. Maplewood (Aldrich Arena 777-1361)...................770-4570

16. Minneapolis (Parade Ice Garden 370-4846)..............661-4875
17. Minnetonka (Ice Arena 939-8310) 939-8200
18. Plymouth (Ice Center) 509-5200
19. Ramsey County (10 indoor arenas) 777-1707
20. Richfield (Ice Arena 861-9351)............................861-9385

21. Roseville (Minnesota Oval 415-2160).....................415-2100
22. St. Louis Park (Recreation Center 924-2545) 924-2540
23. St. Paul (Highland Arena 699-7156) 266-6400
24. White Bear Lake (Sports Center 429-8571) 429-8566
25. Woodbury (Sports Center 458-3301) 731-5788

Ski jumping at the Battle Creek Ski Jump in 1940.

SKI JUMPING

I started skiing when I was five years old and ski jumping was one of the things that originally got me hooked on the sport. Growing up in Vermont, I spent hours jumping in my backyard and tied rope around my bicycle wheels so I could ride over the snowy streets to the jumping hill at the University of Vermont. There I would jump until it was too dark to see the landing hill.

All kids love to jump on skis and often find that feeling of flying even before they learn to turn. It's hard to keep them down on the ground. They seem to know instinctively that a pair of skis is more than just a way of sliding downhill ... it's also a ticket to freedom from the constraints of gravity.

Billy Kidd
Olympic Silver Medalist, 1964
World Alpine Championship Gold Medalist, 1970

This must be the best kept secret in the Twin Cities. No sport, summer or winter, is more dramatic – for spectators and competitors alike. No sport is more suitable for learning at an early age. No other U.S. city has better facilities for training and competition. And no sport has its roots as thoroughly entwined in Minnesota as ski jumping.

By the end of 1997, the Twin Cities will have a brand new K-70 ski jump — big enough for flying over 200 feet through the air. The sleek steel jump will rise above Bush Lake Road in Bloomington at the home base of the Minneapolis Ski Club.

The long, storied history of ski jumping in Minnesota is outlined below, but this isn't a sport that lives in the past. The St. Paul and Minneapolis ski clubs are committed to their youth programs for boys and girls. The St. Paul facility has snowmaking machines in winter and has just installed an artificial surface for jumping in summer.

While the Boomer generation might remember the spectacular fall of jumper Vinko Bogotaj spelling "the agony of defeat" on the opening segment of ABC's *WideWorld of Sports,* they probably don't realize that Vinko escaped serious injury and that ski jumping is less dangerous than downhill skiing. Ski jumpers may travel 150 feet or more (the world record is 686 feet set in 1995 by Epren Bredesen at the "ski flying" hill at Planica, Yugoslavia), but they are rarely more than fifteen feet above the steeply contoured hills.

Norwegians for years, and lately the Finns, have dominated the ski jumping scene at the international level, but Minnesotans have often been at the top nationally. As recently as 1976, six of the seven U.S. Olympic ski jumpers were from here. And the only Olympic medal in ski jumping ever won by an American went to St. Paul Ski Club member Anders Haugen in 1924.

The latest youth movement in local ski jumping has already begun. Time will tell how far these skiers will go. But even if you or your kids never graduate from the sledding hill to the ski jumping hill, you owe it to yourself to get out and watch the action. It's almost as much fun to watch the tykes coming off the bunny hop as it is to see top competitors soaring off the 45-meter jump.

Youngster jumping at Bush Lake "Bunny Hop," 1995.

Courtesy of the Minneapolis Ski Club

HISTORY OF SKI JUMPING

In Minnesota, winter comes to stay. And in the second half of the 19th century so did plenty of Scandinavians. Add in a few big hills and steep bluffs and it's no surprise that Minnesota led the way for ski jumping as a sport in the New World.

North America's first ski club organized in St. Paul on November 30, 1885. The first governed cross country ski meet and ski jumping competition took place on St. Paul's West Side on January 25, 1887, as part of the second Winter Carnival. These events were not simply milestones in America, they were quite early in the entire development of sport skiing. The first ski competitions (for ski running and jumping) open to civilians were held in Tromsoy, Norway, in 1843. The first ski club was organized in Trysil, Norway, in 1861. And the prestigious Holmenkollen ski competitions did not begin until 1892 – five years after St. Paul's landmark event.

Equally remarkable is that the man who almost single-handedly began the modern era of sport skiing moved to Minnesota in 1884 and spent four of his final years here. In the 1850s, Sondre Norheim broke with 7,000 years of skiing tradition by fashioning an osier withe binding that wrapped around the heel and gave him unprecedented control of his skis. He had invented the means and the method for the Telemark Turn, still in use a century and a half later.

Sondre Norheim leaping from a rooftop in Morgedal, Norway.

Sondre Norheim made the first recorded jump – nearly 100 feet! – at Morgedal, his hometown in the Telemark district of Norway, in 1860. In 1868, Norheim and some of his compatriots travelled (by skis, of course) to the city of Christiana (now Oslo) and turned the ski world on its ear with their new jumping style. Theodore Johnson tells the story in his 1905 book, *The Winter Sport of Skeeing.*

> *It is interesting to know how the Telemarken peasants, fresh from their Norway mountain home, first proved to the skeeing enthusiasts of Christiana and the rest of the world that long leaps on skees were not only possible, but practical as well. The races and leaping took place at Huseby, near Christiana, on a slope which has been considered highly dangerous, and even impossible to descend when the snow was fast. It was the leaping competition which proved the most interesting. In this every man except the Telemarkens carried a long staff on which, so they thought, their lives depended. As they slid down the slopes sitting astride their poles like witches on broomsticks and making frantic efforts to check their speed, their appearance was ludicrous in the extreme. Then, at the platform where they were supposed to leap, they merely "trickled" over, landing softly below, and slipped awkwardly on to the foot of the slope.*
>
> *Then came the Telemarken boys. They stood erect, pliant, confident, carrying nothing but a fir branch in their hands. They started with a rush, they gathered speed with every downward foot of their course, and bounding out into the air, cleared seventy-six feet of space ere their skees touched the slippery slope below! Then shooting onward to the plain they suddenly turned, stopped in a smother of snow dust, and faced the hill they had just descended! That was indeed a skeeing revelation to the Christiana experts, and a sight never to be forgotten.*

Sondre Norheim was by now in his mid-forties, but he continued ski jumping and teaching the sport to local boys and girls. His best students were the Hemmestvedt family; their daughter Aasne won one of the first girl's races in Morgedal in 1878. Her two brothers, Mikkel and Torjus, followed Sondre to Minnesota in 1886 and 1888 and set the standard for skiing throughout the Upper Midwest.

Both Mikkel and Torjus had won national championships in long distance (55 kilometer) races and ski jumping events shortly before their arrival. They were at the height of their powers when they arrived here and Mikkel Hemmestvedt joined a hastily formed group of Norman County skiers for that first ski meet on January 25, 1887.

The site of the first meet was on the hill at Halsted Avenue which ran northwest-southeast, just south of today's St. Paul Downtown Airport. Officers from each of the five assembled clubs met and agreed upon a set of rules (most likely based on those used in Norway).

The *Pioneer Press* reported, "a chute 20-feet-high was erected on top of the hill. On the lower hill was formed a precipice that, without any personal effort, sent the runner at least 40 feet out in midair. The race consisted of three runs, two leaps over the precipice, and one over the same route, and continued for one mile. The best time in this race was made by Mikkel Hemestvedt of Ada, Minnesota, who at the last leap jumped more than 60 feet, and made the long run in four minutes and thirty seconds."

Fourteen-year-old Oscar Arentson of Red Wing took first prize in the second class competition. Club members retired to Grote's Tivoli, a popular restaurant, after the tournament. Lunch was served and, in the spirit of the ongoing St. Paul Winter Carnival, the prize winners were "bounced" in the air in a blanket by a ring of men. The celebration continued with toasts and speeches until a late hour.

On February 8, 1887, a second ski jumping tournament was held in Red Wing and Mikkel was again the winner. The Aurora Club of Red Wing sponsored this contest. The club was typically Scandinavian and all club business was conducted in Norwegian. At one meeting it was necessary to remind the secretary, *who had lapsed into English*, that some members did not understand the new language.

The Hemmestvedt brothers local dominance ended in 1893 when Mikkel returned to Norway. At one of their last meets together, Torjus and Mikkel made a memorable demonstration jump. They descended the hill hand-in-hand, leapt and landed together to the joy of all who watched.

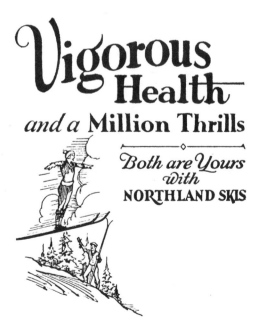

Christian Lund came to St. Paul from Oslo, Norway, and started the Northland Ski Company in 1911. At his own expense, Lund outfitted the U.S. ski team for the first Winter Olympics held in Chomonix, France, in 1924.

St. Paul skier Anders Haugen, jumping at a meet in 1935. Anders is the only U.S. ski jumper to ever win an Olympic medal.

The next ten years saw a series of warm winters and little ski jumping activity. The Winter Carnival was put on hold after its first three glorious years. The Central Ski Organization had disbanded, but on February 22, 1905, a meeting of five midwestern clubs was held that led to the formation of the National Ski Association. The St. Paul Ski Club and Red Wing's Aurora Club were charter members.

By the early part of the century ski jumping tournaments were again held on a regular basis. St. Paul Ski Club secretary Hans Meyer reported a 1908 meet where "several thousand people showed up, and they certainly got their money's worth. This tournament like it's predecessors proved anything but a financial success. It seems against the principles of the St. Paul public to pay anything to see a ski tournament if they, by tearing down a fence or knocking down a policeman, can see it for nothing."

Harriet Island, not known for its steep hills or precipices, was the site of the 1916 ski slide. Built as part of the revived St. Paul Winter Carnival, it generated enough interest that a new steel scaffold was erected at West Seventh and Alaska streets where the National Ski Tournament was held in 1917. A blinding snowstorm did not hold back the reported crowds of 15,000 spectators. It did affect competition as the winning jump of 115 feet was considerably less than the practice jumps. Ole Mangseth finished out of the prize circle and told the *Pioneer Press*, "I take just two looks, one when I leave the top and another just as I jump. Other times I shut my eyes."

In 1919, St. Paul Ski Club member Anders Haugen set a new "World's Record" with a jump of 213 feet in Dillon, Colorado. The Minneapolis Ski Club hosted the 1923 National Championship tournament won by Anders Haugen and in 1924, at the first Winter Olympics, Anders Haugen was the top American jumper and took the bronze medal. Somehow, there was an error in the scoring and this fact went unrecognized for 56 years.

The St. Paul Winter Carnival was revived in 1937 and the third time was a charm as it has continued (except for World War II) ever since. In 1939, the National Ski Jumping Championship was held at the brand new Battle Creek Ski Jump. Norwegian ski star Reidar Andersen established the hill record with a leap of 197 feet. Though it would be matched later, his jump would remain the longest standing jump ever completed in St. Paul.

Tom Harrington, whose name has been enshrined at Harrington Hill where today's St. Paul Ski Club now makes its home, entered his first tournament at Battle Creek in 1941. Tom was the top St. Paul jumper in 1954 and 1959 and served as chair or president of several local and national ski jumping organizations. He is also the author of *On Wings of Wood*, the fascinating history of the St. Paul Ski Club without which this chapter could not have been written.

Efforts to gain publicity for the sport continued after World War II. Minneapolis Ski Club member Henry Hansen turned a somersault from the big Battle Creek Ski Jump in 1950. And in 1953, St. Paul jumpers Roy Ohlson, John Lyons and Gene Lewis completed a daring triple leap from the 60-meter Battle Creek Ski Jump.

The Battle Creek hill record of 197 feet lasted 31 years until 1971 when Tim Denisson tied it twice on the same afternoon. The last tournament at Battle Creek in 1974 turned memorable when 17-year-old Kip Sundgaard thrilled the crowd with two standing jumps of 196 and 197 feet. Kip won the NCAA National Ski Jumping Championship in 1976 and competed in the Olympics. In March of 1969 he soared farther than any Minnesotan before or since with a tremendous leap of 464 feet at Planica, Yugoslavia.

A new era for the St. Paul Ski Club began in December, 1972, with the unveiling of Harrington Hill. The St. Paul Winter Carnival Tournament kicked off with a hill record leap of 144 feet by Minneapolis Olympic team member Jerry Martin on January 26, 1975.

In 1982, the United States Ski Association initiated a Master's Class ski jumping championship for competitors 27 years and older. (Master's III is for skiers 50 years and older.) Harrington Hill hosted the festivities that took a historic bent when 74-year-old Pete Dennison put on a number and took a jump. Pete first jumped during the era when the Hammestvedt brothers were still active. He was there that day to witness one of the brightest new stars when Kip Sundgaard leaped 163 feet – a new hill record and well past the transition zone at the landing area.

The story of ski jumping continues to unfold. To use the older jumpers' own words, here's hoping they "make it long and pretty!"

GETTING STARTED

I crouched, poised on the top of the ramp, looking down the slide. Helmet on, shifting the fat unfamiliar skis below me. Excitement was building, now or never, I took off, gained speed and sprung forward at the lip of the take-off. I flew what, maybe eight feet, ten feet and landed, gliding down the short out-run and stopped. Big smile! Hey, just past 40 and I'd completed my first ski jump.

Beginning ski jumpers start on very small hills. The idea is to learn the basic techniques of jumping, landing and stopping before moving to a larger hill. Ski programs for youth are well coached, equipment is available and kids move up at the rate they feel comfortable with.

In competition, points are scored for both length of jumps (without falling) and style. Nordic combined tournaments include cross country skiing and ski jumping, as they have for over 150 years. Most ski jumpers start quite young – ages 6 to 12 years is common. Teenagers have always been some of the top competitors since 14-year-old Oscar Arentson took the second class prize in the first ski jumping meet held in 1887. On the other hand, there are champions who didn't commit to the sport until their twenties.

Older skiers who want to give the sport a try should call ahead and make arrangements. Both local clubs are amenable to giving interested individuals a chance to try this exciting sport. If you have downhill ski equipment you can use it to start jumping. At least one exceptionally skilled downhill skier, with good coaching, has progressed from the 5-meter to the 30-meter jump in a single night.

While not a lifelong sport in the same sense as cross country skiing, notable elder statesmen in the sport include Dale Severson of North Oaks who won a gold medal at age 60 in the U.S. Masters Championship in 1996.

Courtesy of the Minneapolis Ski Club

Youngsters test their wings at the Bush Lake Ski Jump.

Drawings from Teaching Children to Ski, *Human Kinetics Publishers. Reprinted by permission from A. Flemmen & O. Grosvold, 1982.*

Olympic-hopeful Chris Broz shows fine form at a meet in Coleraine, Minnesota.

View from above of "Flying V" position of skis now used by the best jumpers.

SKI JUMPING CLUBS & EVENTS

Minneapolis Ski Club

Jack Broz, 943-8956
9550 Garrison Way
Eden Prairie, MN 55347
Jay Martin – jumping division of club, 425-7511

BUSH LAKE SKI JUMP, located at 84th and East Bush Lake Road in Bloomington, just north of Hyland Hills. See map on page 52.

The roots of the Minneapolis Ski Club are nearly as deep and storied as that of the St. Paul Ski Club chronicled above – it's just not as well documented. Started in 1886, the Minneapolis Ski Club sports some 400 to 500 members of which about 20% take part in ski jumping. The club also embraces cross country ski racing, nordic combined (jumping and racing) and biathlon training and competition (cross country skiing and target shooting!).

Completion of the new 70-K jump in late 1997 is sure to put the Minneapolis Ski Club in the bright lights again. The club hosts several events each year at their ski jumping facility at Bush Lake. The season kicks off with the annual **Snow Bowl** tournament on New Year's Eve and continues through their **Evergreen** meet on the first Sunday in March.

St. Paul Ski Club

LeeAnn Myhra, 426-8506
9406 75th Street North
Stillwater, MN 55082

HARRINGTON HILL SKI JUMP, phone 739-1285, located in Maplewood. Take Hwy. 61 south 4 miles from I-94 and turn left (east) at Carver Avenue. Continue up Carver and just before the I-494 underpass take Sterling St. left (north) to entrance.

The oldest club in America has one of the country's best youth programs. The season begins with its annual training camp between Christmas and New Year's and the club hosts tournaments every Friday night through early March. The **St. Paul Classic** is one of their major annual tourneys.

The St. Paul Ski Club has a beautiful, year-round facility with a chalet (refreshments, meeting rooms and washrooms), four jumping hills, lights, snowmaking and summer jumping surface. The club is easing back into developing a cross country skiing program and is forming a women's division.

Children sliding down a hill in 1940.

SLEDDING & SNOW TUBING

Nothing put a bigger smile on my face last winter than my first time tubing out at Eko Backen.

If you're feeling a little glum. Bored. Down in the mouth. Here's the cure. Find something slippery to sit on, and head for the hills.

Sledding, tubing, tobogganing and sliding are all low on skills and high on thrills. The key is to pick a good line downhill, make sure it's relatively free of other sliding bodies, and jump on. Oh yeah — hang on tight!

One of the great aspects of tubing versus other sliding apparatus is that the tubes are big shock absorbers. You can get airborne quite easily on the bigger hills but landing on a soft tube cushions the impact.

Feet first, head first, on your stomach, on your back — you choose. Everything short of standing straight up and beating on your chest as you scream downhill works fine.

HISTORY

Sliding down hills for winter entertainment must go back as far as there have been people living in northern climates.

In Minnesota, tobogganing has a well-documented history as part of the St. Paul Winter Carnival. The very first carnival in 1886 featured a six-track toboggan course near today's State Capitol.

At the 1888 carnival it was reported that, "staid bank presidents are found sitting in their offices in full toboggan uniform." A huge toboggan slide ran down Ramsey Hill in 1917. For just a quarter you could take a ride from the top of Ramsey Street at Summit Avenue down 1,500 feet to Seven Corners. In 1996, over 50 tons of snow were used to build a 200-foot toboggan slide below the State Capitol. Giant sculptures of King Boreas and Vulcanus Rex smiled down on the proceedings.

St. Paul's Northland Ski Company was a major manufacturer of wood toboggans for decades. In 1992, Minnesotan Craig Kruckeberg started building toboggans from 100% recycled plastic milk jugs. The MJ Hummer toboggan that resulted took a first place at the U.S. National Toboggan Championships in 1995.

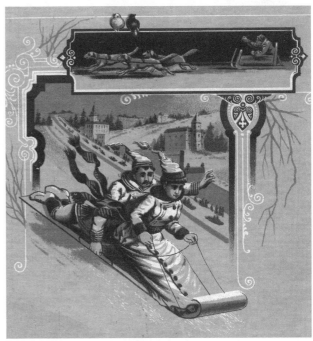

Engraving from the 1888 St. Paul Winter Carnival.

Private collection

GETTING STARTED

Like everything else, sledding is not nearly as simple as it was when I was a child in the sixties. Back then there were sliding hills where everything from spiffy, steel-bladed sleds to cardboard sheets were perfectly fine.

Now, in the great old United States of Litigation, there are often rules about what is allowed (tubes, plastic discs) and what is not (steel-bladed sleds, toboggans, snowboards, etc.). When I was calling around to find out where the good sledding hills were located, more than a few municipalities declined to acknowledge any, and I know of a couple of instances (e.g., Lochness Park in Blaine) where a hill is now posted *No Sledding.*

Kids always seem to find the best local spots anyway. Besides the neighborhood hills, there are now seven metro tubing hills, plus a toboggan slide that opened at Oak Hill in St. Louis Park in 1996.

SLIDING HILLS

Hennepin Parks has great sledding hills at several locations.

Most of the hills listed below are not overly discriminating on the types of sleds they allow. Hennepin Parks is picky, so leave the flexible flyers and toboggans at home. Call in advance if you have any questions about what is allowed, hours (beyond daylight) they are open and if a warming house or other amenities are available.

Sliding hills located in parks with cross country skiing (e.g., **Baker Park Reserve**) often have more complete facilities. These are fully described and mapped in the CROSS COUNTRY SKIING chapter. Cities listed below with phone numbers are not described in that chapter.

1. **Anoka County Trails** – Hill at Bunker Hills Regional Park

2. **Baker Park Reserve**

3. **Battle Creek Regional Park** – Hill on Winthrop Street

4. **Bloomington Trails** – Running and Brookside Parks

5. **Brooklyn Park,** phone 493-8333. Several hills including Bass Creek Park (6700 Boone Av.), Central Park (8440 Regent) and Hartkopf Park (73rd and Douglas).

6. **Burnsville,** phone 895-4500. Hills at Northview Park (Co. Rd. 5 and 155th Street), Neill Park (Burnsville Parkway and Upton Avenue), and North River Hills.

7. **Carver County Trails** – Hill at Baylor Regional Park

8. **Carver Park Reserve**

9. **Como Park** – Check out 1,000-foot-long Robbinson's Bowl next to the ski area

10. **Coon Rapids,** phone 767-6462. Wintercrest (Magnolia and 101st Avenue) is the most popular, but Rockslide and Peppermint Stick sound tempting.

11. **Eagan Trails** – Hills at Blackhawk Park and Trapp Farm (see "Snow Tubing" section).

12. **Eden Prairie,** phone 949-8442. Sledding at Forest Hills Park (off Baker Road) and Staring Lake Park (see "Snow Tubing" section).

13. **Elm Creek Park Reserve**

14. **French Regional Park**

15. **Frontenac State Park**

16. **Hoffman Hills State Park,** Menomonie, Wisconsin

17. **Hyland Park Reserve**

18. **Inver Grove Heights,** phone 450-2585. Hills at North Valley and South Valley Parks (off 70th Street, east of Cahill Avenue).

19. **Kinnickinnick State Park**

20. **Lake Maria State Park**

21. **Maplewood,** phone 770-4570. Playcrest Park (2390 Lydia, at McKnight Road) has a hill.

22. **Mille Lacs Kathio State Park**

Cedar Street toboggan slide at the St. Paul Winter Carnival in 1917.

Photograph by A.F. Raymond, Minnesota Historical Society Collections

23. **Minneapolis,** phone 661-4875. Lots of great hills at Beard's Plaisance (SW corner of Lake Harriet), Bryant Avenue and 40th Street, Columbia Golf Course, Powderhorn Park (35th Street and 15th Avenue) and **Wirth Park**.

24. **Oakdale,** phone 730-2702. Hill at Oakdale Park 42 (off 45th Street, east of Century Avenue).

25. **Plymouth,** phone 509-5200. Several hills including those at Lacompte Park (Co. Rd. 15 near Hwy. 55), Rolling Hills (48th and Saratoga) and Zachary Park (4355 Zachary Lane).

26. **Ramsey County Trails** – Hills at Keller Golf Course, Manitou Ridge Golf Course and Snail Lake Regional Park.

27. **Richfield,** phone 861-9385. Hill at Augsburg Park (70th and Nicollet).

28. **Sunfish Lake Park**

29. **St. Louis Park** phone 924-2540. Bobsled run at Oak Hill Park (see "Snow Tubing" section).

30. **St. Paul,** phone 266-6400. Sensational sliding at Baker Park (Page St. east of Smith Av.), Como Park, Highland Park (Snelling Av. and Ford Parkway), Indian Mounds (Earl and Mounds Blvd.) and Town and Country Club (private club at 2279 Marshall Av. with view of Minneapolis skyline).

31. **Wirth Park** – A great sledding hill for the generations, plus snow tubing hill (see next section).

Courtesy of Craig Kruckeberg

Geno Boyd, Cedric Boyd and Craig Kruckeberg (left to right), plus Kevin Hart, piloted the 100% recycled plastic MJ Hummer Toboggan to a U.S. National Tobogganing title in 1995. This ultrafast toboggan is made in Minnesota. Phone 800-248-3855.

Photo by Nancy Conroy, courtesy of Minneapolis Parks Board

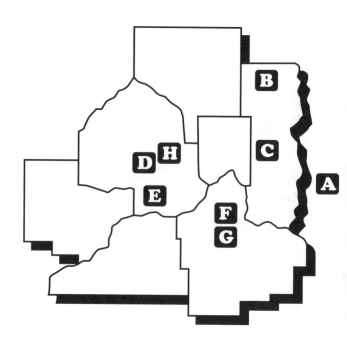

Map of Twin Cities' snow tubing locations described below.

Snow tubing and tobogganing are certainly more entertainment than sport. Half of the places listed here have rope tows that haul you back up the hill so the truly lazy need hardly get off their butts all day.

This is great fun for kids of all ages. Places with rope tows have an admission fee and tubes or toboggans are included in the price. Most places have group discounts for parties of 20 or more.

A. BADLANDS, HUDSON, WI

Phone 715-386-1856 or 715-386-2216

GO! Take I-94 east to exit #4 and go left (north) 1 mile. Take a right (east) on Badlands Road and go 2 miles to Kinney Road, then right (south) on Kinney to entrance.

Hours Fri. 7 pm to 10 pm, Sat. 10 to 10 pm, Sun. noon to 10 pm

Admission $5 Friday night, $7 to $9 weekends

Facilities Four slopes, two rope tows, chalet in an old farmhouse with pizza, pop, sandwiches, cider, etc.

B. EKO BACKEN, FOREST LAKE

Phone 433-2422

GO! Take I-35E or 35W north and exit at Hwy. 97. Go right (east) 6 miles to Manning (Co. Rd. 15) and left (north) 1.5 miles on Manning to entrance.

Hours Open 6:30 pm to 10 pm weekdays and 11 am to 10 pm weekends and holidays

Admission $6.50 (12 and under), $7.50 (13 and older)

Facilities Two-story chalet with game room and bar overlooks the three slopes and two rope tows. Hot dogs, nachos, pizza and pop. Snowmaking and sleigh rides.

Tobogganing at Glenwood (Wirth) Park in 1925. Courtesy of Minneapolis Parks Board.

Fred cruises down the big hill at Eko Backen.

C. GREEN ACRES, LAKE ELMO

Phone 770-6060

GO! Take Hwy. 36 1.5 miles east of I-694 and then right (south) on Demontreville Trail (Co. Rd. 13) ¹/4 mile to entrance.

Hours Two-hour sessions Fri. (5:30 and 8), Sat. (12:30, 3, 5:30 and 8) and Sun. (12:30, 3 and 5:30)

Admission $7.50 (12 and under), $9 (13 and older)

Facilities Large chalet with pool table and game room plus cheeseburgers, hot chocolate, sodas, etc. Former downhill ski area. Must be 13-years-old to ride the big hill, which usually opens in late December. Snowmaking.

D. OAK HILL, ST. LOUIS PARK

Phone 924-2540

GO! Take Minnetonka Blvd. west 1.5 miles from Hwy. 100 to Rhode Island Av. Turn left (south) 4 blocks to entrance.

Hours Fri. to Sun. and Christmas break noon to 10 pm

Admission Toboggan (holds 1 to 2) rental is $1.

Facilities The area's only toboggan slide has three tracks and a warming house with concessions. Ten thousand colored tree lights decorate the scene, and the park also has open skating (rental skates, $1) and a sledding hill.

E. STARING LAKE, EDEN PRAIRIE

Phone 949-8442 or 949-8445   See page 64 and 65.

GO! Take Hwy. 212 southwest from I-494 to Pioneer Trail. Turn right (west) and go 1 mile to entrance on right.

Hours Mon. to Thurs. 4 to 8, Fri. 4 to 9:30, Sat. 10 to 9:30, Sun. noon to 8 pm

Admission Free tubes! No metal sleds or plastic toboggans.

Facilities Warming house with pop, washrooms and fireplace. Groomed 700-foot-long sliding hill plus skating.

F. TRAPP FARM PARK, EAGAN

Phone 681-4660   See page 43.

GO! Exit Cedar Avenue or I-35E at Diffley Road and go east to Lexington Avenue. Turn right (south) and go to Wilderness Run Road. Turn left (east) and go 6 blocks to entrance.

Hours Mon. to Thurs. 4 to 8, Fri. 4 to 9:30, Sat. 10 to 9:30, Sun. noon to 8 pm

Admission Free tubes! Metal runners and plastic toboggans prohibited.

Facilities Warming house with washrooms, fireplace and hot chocolate.

G. VALLEYWOOD GOLF COURSE, APPLE VALLEY

Phone 953-2300

GO! Take Pilot Knob Road south from I-35E 4 miles to 125th Street (Co. Rd. 38). Turn left (east) ¹/4 mile to entrance on left.

Hours Open weekends 10 to 5 pm

Admission Free. Tube rental $2/hour, sleds OK

Facilities Clubhouse not always available. Cross country skiing is allowed but no groomed trails are provided.

H. WIRTH PARK, MINNEAPOLIS

Phone 522-4584   See page 82.

GO! Take Golden Valley Road east from Hwy. 100 1.5 miles to Wirth Pkwy. Turn right (south) and go ¹/2 mile to entrance at Plymouth Ave.

Hours Open Thurs. and Fri. 5 to 9 pm, Sat. 10 to 9, Sun. 1 to 7:30 pm

Admission $2 (17 and under), $4 (adults), $5 deposit

Facilities Swiss-style chalet with fireplace, washrooms and food. One big hill with rope tow.

SNOWSHOEING

On January 13, 1982, wilderness writer Sigurd Olson went out into the woods one last time. He was trying out a new pair of snowshoes and was exploring a little wooded valley a short ways from his Ely, Minnesota, home. It was there he passed away.

Before going out on this last small hike he stepped into his writing cabin and wrote his final words. On a white sheet of paper he typed a single line. "A new adventure is coming up and I know it will be a good one."

If you can walk, you can snowshoe. Better yet, consider this: "In 20 minutes you can be an expert," says Dyke Williams. He should know. His company makes traditional Ojibwa snowshoes and Williams has led snowshoe trips for nearly three decades. In snowshoeing, proper technique simply means not falling down.

In the past four or five years, a whole new world of snowshoeing has developed with the advent of "modern" snowshoe construction. Like skate skiing in the world of cross country, these new "modern" snowshoes have changed the face of snowshoeing. They are smaller, lighter (only about two pounds!), and can be used with running shoes, boots or mukluks. Designs are available for all snow conditions.

Modern snowshoes have brought a whole new crowd — runners and walkers — into the sport as a way to extend their season. These snowshoes can also give a better workout in a shorter time, and snowshoeing is less jarring on the body than running.

Although the new lightweight shoes have attracted many new snowshoers, it would be a mistake to think that it's time to hang up the traditional wood designs. (They do look nice above the fireplace though.) The centuries-old Ojibwa snowshoe design still works fine. They are built to last a lifetime.

Either way, snowshoeing is a low-impact aerobic activity that can allow you to more safely navigate nearby paths or let you explore the wildest terrain Minnesota has to offer. Snowshoes are easy to use and relatively inexpensive. A good pair of traditional or modern snowshoes can be purchased for $130 to $250.

The resurgence of showshoeing as both a sport and recreation has led to greatly expanded opportunities for competition (See "Snowshoeing Events" section) and just plain beating around the bush.

A park naturalist leads a couple of youngsters on a snowshoe hike at Fort Snelling State Park.

RACE BETWEEN THE COLUMBIA AND THE ST. GEORGE'S SNOW SHOE CLUB.

Snowshoe competition depicted in the Carnival Edition, St. Paul Dispatch, *January 16, 1887.*

SNOWSHOEING HISTORY

About 6,000 years ago, evidence indicates that primitive snowshoes were made in Central Asia for easier travel over snow. Some people have suggested that this innovation allowed these early people to migrate into North America via the Bering Strait. But archaeologists know that people have been living in Minnesota for some 10,000 years, and one could speculate that American Indians have used some form of snowshoe for at least as long as the Asians.

The snowshoe has been in use by traditional people from time immemorial. The shape it took varied by location. The Alaskan snowshoe is large and long for trail use in deep snow. Green Mountain Bearpaws are short and oval-shaped for working in close quarters or on more mountainous terrain.

The Ojibwa snowshoe is named after the American Indians who have lived in northern Minnesota and the Great Lakes region for generations. It is perfectly suited to winter travel in this area.

The use of snowshoes purely for recreation began in Canada, where the Montreal Snow Shoe Club formed around 1840. The first St. Paul Winter Carnival in 1886 produced the first local snowshoe clubs. These claimed to be the first U.S. clubs to be formed.

The 1887 Carnival Edition of the *St. Paul Dispatch* said there were half a dozen clubs in the city with about 200 members. The Columbia, St. George and Seven Corners Snow Shoe clubs were among the first groups formed. The *Dispatch* reported that "the clubs take their run of a half dozen miles or so, beguiling themselves the while with snow shoe songs. Woodruff Hall, at Merriam Park, is the resort for the snowshoers when on the tramp."

The official program for the 1888 St. Paul Winter Carnival indicated that snowshoeing had reached its zenith. It exclaimed that, "some

idea of the zeal shown by the citizens may be gleaned from the fact that there are nearly one hundred organized toboggan and snowshoe clubs in St. Paul, comprising nearly 10,000 uniformed ladies and gentlemen."

Mild winters through the 1890s led to the demise of the Winter Carnival, and with it, the large, active snowshoe clubs. While community snowshoe hikes remained popular in New England until the early 1930s, there is no indication of similar activity here. Winter photos of the *Minnehiker Municipal Hiking Club* (See WINTER WALKING chapter) that formed in 1920 reveal boots but no snowshoes on their regular winter outings.

The renaissance of cross country skiing in the 1970s and early 1980s got people thinking about other ways of self-propelled winter travel. The advent of lightweight, maneuverable modern snowshoes has seen the sport take off. The new shoes have led to a resurgence of snowshoeing events — guided nature walks, winter hikes and races that keep growing in popularity. Participation has doubled for three straight years.

GETTING STARTED

Hennepin Parks (559-9000) has an annual **Snowshoe Festival** in early January each year. Several modern and traditional snowshoe manufacturers are on hand with equipment you can try out. There are also many parks where you can rent snowshoes or use them as part of a program. See "Oh, The Places You'll Go!" section.

Midwest Mountaineering (339-3433) has an annual **Winterfest** in early November with lots of information on the latest in snowshoes, places to go and upcoming events.

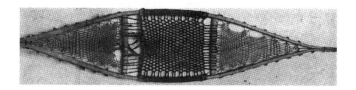

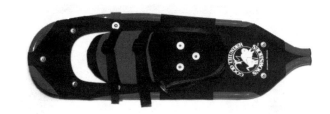

TRADITIONAL SNOWSHOES

These designs are the end result of some 6,000 years of snowshoe development and improvement. The Ojibwa snowshoe is made with white ash frames and varnished rawhide or (preferably) tubular nylon lacing. An American Indian-made snowshoe is shown above.

BINDINGS — The modified "H" binding in neoprene works well. The "A" binding also has advocates.

LOCAL MANUFACTURER — Wilcox and Williams
Phone 929-4935

DRESS FOR SUCCESS

- Finally, a sport where lycra outfits are not de rigueur.
- See the chapter, WELCOME TO WINTER, Dress for Success.
- Snowshoes, especially when running, kick up snow onto your back side. Gore-Tex pants will help.
- Running shoes, hiking boots, mukluks and Sorels can all be used.
- Bring an old ski pole (or two) with a big basket for better balance.
- Binoculars, birding guides and animal tracking books are useful additions to your pack.

OH, THE PLACES YOU'LL GO!

> *Leave the beaten track occasionally and dive into the woods. You will be certain to find something that you have never seen before.*
>
> **Alexander Graham Bell**

There are dozens of places to go snowshoeing nearby. Many of these are mapped and described in the CROSS COUNTRY SKIING chapter and referenced below. For the more adventurous, there are literally hundreds of miles of frozen rivers and creeks in the metro area just waiting to be explored. Be careful!

The largest stretch of undeveloped land in the metro area is the **Carlos Avery Wildlife Management Area** which straddles northern Anoka and Chisago counties. It contains 23,000 acres of marsh, grasslands and woods. It is mostly level, and can be skied as well. A bear was found hibernating here in 1996. Phone 296-5290 or 296-3344 for a map or directions.

MODERN SNOWSHOES

These new snowshoes are smaller, lighter, more maneuverable and a lot of fun. Made with aluminum and metal alloy frames and synthetics, they "float" well on deeper snow and work fine on most trails for jogging or running. The Good Thunder "Lightening" model with insulated "Hot Action" binding is shown above.

BINDINGS — Insulated bindings are available to help keep feet warm.

LOCAL MANUFACTURER — Good Thunder Snowshoes
Phone 824-2385

The following nature centers have naturalist-led snowshoe hikes (snowshoes are provided) at least a couple of times each winter. There is a small charge and advance registrations must be made by phone. These places are generally run by foundations and this is often the only way the public can visit them.

Carpenter St. Croix Valley Nature Center
In Washington County, phone 437-4359. Two moonlight snowshoe hikes followed by refreshments indoors.

Lee and Rose Warner Nature Center
In Washington County, phone 433-2427. Open one Saturday each month in winter for naturalist-led snowshoe hikes that go through a unique bog area.

Thomas Irvine Dodge Nature Center
In West St. Paul, phone 455-4531. Showshoe hikes on Saturdays in January and early February.

Westwood Hills Nature Center
In St. Louis Park, phone 924-2544. Snowshoe hikes with refreshments on Sunday afternoons in January.

MORE PLACES TO GO SNOWSHOEING

See CROSS COUNTRY SKIING chapter for map and description of each area. The following list describes places that have snowshoe programs, **rental** and designated trails or areas. *All other parks and trails, except those noted at the end of this section, allow snowshoeing but you must stay off ski trails.*

There is good terrain for snowshoeing (off the ski trails!) at Afton, Banning, Fort Snelling, Frontenac, William O'Brien and Willow River State Parks. The Minnesota River Trail (Bloomington Trails) and Louisville Swamp are also good choices.

1. **Anoka County Trails** – allowed anywhere but ski trails.
   a. **Coon Rapids Dam Regional Park** – Hennepin Parks Visitor Center (424-8172), **rental**, 4-kilometer trail.
   b. **Wargo Nature Center** (429-8007) at Rice Creek Chain of Lakes has snowshoe programs, **rental** and 1.5 mile trail.
2. **Arcola Trail** – good snowshoe area.
3. **Baker Park Reserve** – designated 100-acre snowshoe exploration area and **rental**.
4. **Carver Park Reserve** – Lowry Nature Center (472-4911) has naturalist-led snowshoe hikes, **rental** and 6-mile trail.
5. **Como Park** – designated "40 acres" area. See map.
6. **Elm Creek Park Reserve** – Eastman Nature Center (420-4300) has programs, naturalist, **rental** and 4-mile trail.
7. **French Regional Park** – naturalist-led (only!) snowshoe hikes (snowshoes provided) to active beaver lodges or lagoons.

8. **Hyland Lake Park Reserve** – Richardson Nature Center (941-7993) has programs, **rental** and 3-mile trail.
9. **Interstate Park,** Wisconsin – naturalist-led hikes (snowshoes provided). Reservations required.
10. **Lake Maria State Park** – packed snow, 3-mile trail.
11. **Lebanon Hills Regional Park** – 9.2-mile packed snow trail.
12. **Mille Lacs Kathio State Park** – naturalist-led trips on special, winter-only trails, moonlight trips and **rental**.
13. **North Hennepin Regional Trail** – Flat, 7-mile packed trail.
14. **Ramsey County Trails** – allowed at Tamarack Nature Center (429-7787) where they have designated area and **rental**.
15. **Richfield Trails** – preregistered naturalist-led hikes (snowshoes included) at Wood Lake Nature Center.
16. **Sherburne National Wildlife Refuge** – There are 31,000 acres to explore.
17. **Wild River State Park** – naturalist-led hikes (snowshoes included) on Saturdays. **Rental** available otherwise.
18. **Wirth Park** – **Rental** and interesting terrain.

Snowshoeing is not allowed at:

Cleary Lake Regional Park	Minnesota Landscape Arboretum
Cottage Grove Ravine Reg. Park	Minnesota Zoo
Crow-Hassan Regional Park	Murphy Hanrehan Park Reserve
Eagan Trails	Phalen-Keller Regional Park
French Regional Park	Pine Point Rock
Lake Elmo Park Reserve	Sunfish Lake Park

SNOWSHOEING EVENTS

WINTERFEST
Second week in November
Sponsored by Midwest Mountaineering (339-3433), this three-day expo features the latest equipment and lectures on all aspects of winter recreation.

SNOWSHOE FESTIVAL
First Saturday in January
Co-sponsored by Hennepin Parks (559-9000), this event offers an excellent chance to try out the latest snowshoe gear.

GOOD THUNDER SNOWSHOE RACES
Weekend days – January, February
Sponsored by the local modern snowshoe manufacturer Good Thunder Snowshoes (824-2385), races range from 5 kilometers to the 100-kilometer Superior Challenge.

JOHN BEARGREASE SNOWSHOE CHAMPIONSHIPS
End of January, Duluth
First run in 1991, the race has separate categories for traditional and modern snowshoes. Lengths range from 5 kilometers to a full marathon (26.2 miles). Phone 824-2385.

Courtesy of Roger Dupey

Kris and Roger Dupey, owners of Good Thunder Snowshoes, out for a run.

There are 225 miles of plowed, paved paths to walk in the metro area. There are miles of frozen stream beds as well — like this one below frozen Minnehaha Falls.

WINTER WALKING

Walking is the most popular form of outside recreation. In winter, walkers and runners often had to endure less than ideal conditions but the picture is rapidly brightening. Many local parks departments have responded to the rising demand for winter walking. This book locates and describes over 200 miles of plowed, paved paths and over 100 miles of packed snow trails. Walkers now have plenty of options to keep them away from the tracked ski trails.

Hennepin Parks' **Southwest Regional LRT Trails** (See map on page 65 or call Hennepin Parks at 559-9000.) have several miles of packed snow trails for walking through Hopkins, Minnetonka, Deephaven, Excelsior and Eden Prairie. The beautiful new **Big Rivers Regional Trail** (map on page 46 or call 438-4662) has a 4.5 mile packed snow trail along the Mississippi River through Mendota. The **Luce Line State Trail** (phone 772-7935) is used more for walking than skiing along the seven miles through Plymouth, Wayzata and Orono. See "Oh, The Places You'll Go!" for a complete list of winter walking opportunities.

HISTORY OF WALKING

Well, this probably parallels the history of humanity.

Two local walking clubs recently celebrated their 75th anniversaries. The Minnehikers, or Minneapolis Municipal Hiking Club, took its first official hike on January 10, 1920. A group of 83 led by Minneapolis Mayor J.E. Meyers and Parks Superintendent Theodore Wirth walked from Minnehaha Falls along the Mississippi to Riverside Park. The path was specially plowed (as it is today) for the group and they enjoyed a bonfire, coffee and donuts at the end of their hike.

The idea of a hiking club sprang from Wirth who later explained,

> *"On a lovely winter morning, I drove from Lake Harriet to Minnehaha Park. The ground and trees were covered with a pure white blanket of fresh-fallen snow. The effect of the early morning sun on the feathery masses of that winter landscape was beautiful beyond description. I wished that every man, woman and child could see the beauties of Minnehaha Parkway that morning. Yet I did not meet one single soul the entire distance of that six-mile drive. Upon my arrival at the office, I told our Mr. Frank C. Berry that we should find some means by which to lead the people to the enjoyment of nature. So he set about and organized the Hiking Club."*

First hike, January 10, 1920. Minnehaha Falls to Riverside Park.

WALKING CLUBS

The first two clubs have relaxed weekly hikes through the winter. Check the Sunday *Pioneer Press* events calendar in the sports section for meeting times and locations. The **Minnesota Orienteering Club** has monthly outdoor events year-round. The **Minnesota Rovers Outing Club** (257-7324) includes winter walking as part of their repertoire and the Wednesday Wanderers in the **North Star Ski Club** (924-9922) hike or ski through winter depending on the weather.

Minneapolis Municipal Hiking Club
Minnehikers c/o MPRB
400 S. 4th Street, Minneapolis, MN 55415
Phone 661-4875
The oldest hiking club in the area can always use new blood. A one-year membership ($11) includes a monthly bulletin.

St. Paul Hiking Club
Phone 644-7502 or 739-4031
The Capitol City club meets twice weekly for outdoor hikes around the metro area.

Minnesota Orienteering Club
P.O. Box 580030, Minneapolis, MN 55458
Phone 553-2848
An exciting year-round sport that sharpens your map and compass skills while you get in shape. Membership includes a newsletter.

OH, THE PLACES YOU'LL GO WALKING!

St. Paul, Minneapolis and most inner-ring suburbs have extensive sidewalk systems that are shoveled by residents. Minneapolis and St. Paul also plow their paths along rivers and lakes for walking in a more natural setting.

The following list summarizes where you can go winter walking in the metro area. Refer to the CROSS COUNTRY SKIING chapter for a map and description of most of these areas. If a phone number is listed, there is not a map for that place in this book. Plowed paths are always paved.

1. **Afton State Park** – one-mile plowed, paved path.
2. **Anoka County Trails** – Bunker Hills Regional Park has a 5.5 mile plowed path, while Coon Rapids Dam Regional Park has a three-mile plowed path.
3. **City of Apple Valley** (953-2300) has several miles of plowed, paved paths.
4. **Battle Creek Regional Park** – 1.5-mile plowed path.
5. **Bloomington Trails** – Normandale Lake has a two-mile plowed path. Girard Lake has a one-mile wood chip trail.
6. **City of Brooklyn Center** (569-3400) has six miles of plowed paths.
7. **City of Burnsville** (895-4500) has four parks, including Sunset Pond, with plowed paths.
8. **Carver Park Reserve** – has a six-mile packed snow trail.
9. **Como Regional Park** – plowed 1.7-mile path around Como Lake plus free zoo and conservatory.
10. **City of Eden Prairie** (949-8442) has over 50 miles of plowed, paved paths.
11. **Elm Creek Park Reserve** – four-mile packed snow trail.
12. **Fort Snelling State Park** – three-mile packed snow trail on Pike Island and 7.8-mile packed snow trail across the river.
13. **Frontenac State Park** – walking allowed on lightly used 12-mile snowmobile trail.
14. **Gateway State Trail** – nine miles of paved, plowed path from St. Paul to I-694, plus a 9.7-mile packed snow path (not the ski trail!) east to Pine Point Park.
15. **Hyland Lake Regional Park** – two-mile packed snow trail.

16. **Interstate Park, Wisconsin** – about four miles of plowed, lightly-used park road.
17. **Lake Elmo Park Reserve** – over three miles of paved, plowed roads closed to cars.
18. **City of Lakeville** (985-4600) – perhaps 10 miles of paths are plowed near schools.
19. **Lake Maria State Park** – packed snow, three-mile (round-trip) trail.
20. **Lebanon Hills Park Reserve** – a separate 9.2-mile packed trail (not the ski trail!) is available.
21. **City of Maplewood** (770-4570) has eight miles of plowed, paved paths.
22. **Minneapolis Trails** – over 26 miles of lake and riverside paths are shoveled or swept daily. These are shared with bicyclists and in-line skaters.
23. **Minnesota Landscape Arboretum** – Three Mile Drive is plowed and closed to cars.
24. **Minnesota Zoo** – the Northern Trail has tigers and camels, or head indoors to the Tropics Trail.
25. **Minnetonka Trails** – over 32 miles of plowed, paved paths.
26. **Murphy Hanrehan** – walking allowed on 3.7-mile horse trail.
27. **Nerstrand Woods State Park** – lightly used 4.5-mile snowmobile trail is available.
28. **Phalen Regional Park** – three-mile plowed path around Lake Phalen.
29. **City of Plymouth** (509-5200) has several miles of plowed, paved paths.
30. **Ramsey County Trail** – Tamarack Nature Center has a 1.1-mile plowed path and Long Lake Reg. Park has a 2-mile path.
31. **St. Paul Trails** (266-6400) – several miles of plowed, paved paths along the Mississippi River, Lake Como and Lake Phalen.
32. **Red Wing Trails** – Barn Bluff is a spectacular hike during low snow winters. Be very careful as the trail can be icy.
33. **Richfield Trails** – Wood Lake Nature Center has a three-mile packed snow trail.
34. **Roseville Trails** – Central Park has a two-mile plowed path around Bennett Lake.
35. **Wild River State Park** – lightly used four-mile (one way) park road available.
36. **Woodbury Trails** – over 35 miles of plowed, paved paths.

INDEX TO PARKS, TRAILS & SKI SLOPES

CHAPTER, **Major Park or Trail**, Park or Trail, *Downhill Ski Area*   Weather on page 11, forecast call 375-0830, snow depth report, 296-5029

St. Paul Winter Carnival —
last week of January, phone 223-4700

EAST METRO WINTER RECREATION

See inside front cover for WEST METRO WINTER RECREATION

7 **PARK** or **TRAIL** CROSS COUNTRY SKIING See pages 16 to 83

NOTE: 1 kilometer (km) = .62 miles (mi)

Z **DOWNHILL SKIING** See pages 84 to 97

SLEDDING (pages 114 to 119), SKATING (pages 102 to 107)

SNOWSHOEING (pages 120 to 123), WINTER CAMPING

BIRD WATCHING (pages 12 to 15), ICE CLIMBING (pages 98 and 99)

WALKING PATHS (pages 124 to 126) and SKI JUMPING (pages 108 to 113)

DAY TRIPS

PARKS and TRAILS (See map on right)

1 AFTON STATE PARK (pg. 27) 32 km ski 1 mi walk

2 ANOKA COUNTY TRAILS (pg. 28) 10 km ski

3 ARCOLA TRAILS (pg. 30) 6 km ski

6 BATTLE CREEK REGIONAL PARK (pg. 33) 14 km ski 1.5 mi walk

13 COMO PARK (pg. 40) 7 km ski 2 mi walk

14 COTTAGE GROVE RAVINE REG. PARK (pg. 41) 11.3 km ski

16 EAGAN SKI TRAILS (pg. 43) 4.8 km ski 1 mi walk
Blackhawk Park   Patrick Eagan Park   Trapp Farm

19 FORT SNELLING PARK (pg. 46) 16.6 km ski 10.8 mi walk
BIG RIVERS REGIONAL TRAIL

22 GATEWAY STATE TRAIL (pg. 49) 15.5 km ski, 18.7 mi walk

23 HIDDEN FALLS REGIONAL PARK (pg. 50) 16 km ski
Highland Nine Hole Ski Area   2 mi walk

28 LAKE ELMO PARK RESERVE (pg. 55) 19 km ski, 3 mi walk

31 LEBANON HILLS REG. PARK (pg. 58) 27.8 km ski
Thompson County Park   9.2 mi walk

35 MINNESOTA ZOO (pg. 63) 10 km ski, 1.5 mi walk

39 PHALEN-KELLER REGIONAL PARK (pg. 68) 16.7 km ski 3 mi walk

40 PINE POINT PARK (pg. 69) 8 km ski

41 PINE TREE APPLE ORCHARD (pg. 70) 10 km ski

42 RAMSEY COUNTY TRAILS (pg. 71) 17.2 km ski
Manitou Ridge Golf Course   1.1 mi walk
Snail Lake Regional Park
Tamarack Nature Center   Oakdale Park

46 ROSEVILLE TRAILS (pg. 75) 7.7 km ski 2 mi walk
Acorn Park   Central Park
Cedarholm Golf Course   Harriet Alexander Nature Center

48 SPRING LAKE PARK RESERVE (pg. 77) 7.4 km ski

49 SUNFISH LAKE PARK (pg. 78) 13.1 km ski

51 WILLIAM O'BRIEN PARK (pg. 80) 19 km ski

54 WOODBURY TRAILS (pg. 83) 7.8 km ski 35 mi walk
Carver Lake Park
Ojibway Park
Tamarack Nature Preserve

DAY TRIPS (See map above)

5 BANNING STATE PARK (pg. 32) 19.3 km ski

9 CANNON VALLEY TRAIL (pg. 36) 34.7 km ski

21 FRONTENAC STATE TRAIL (pg. 48) 12.8 km ski 12 mi walk

24 HOFFMAN HILLS STATE PARK, WIS (pg. 51) 14.7 km ski 1 mi walk

26 INTERSTATE PARK, WIS (pg. 53) 17.8 km ski 4 mi walk

27 KINNICKINNICK STATE PARK, WIS (pg. 54) 10 km ski, 2 mi walk

43 RED WING EAST END TRAILS (pg. 72) 19 km ski, 2 mi walk

50 WILD RIVER STATE PARK (pg. 79) 56 km ski 4 mi walk

52 WILLOW RIVER STATE PARK, WIS (pg. 81) 16 km ski, 1 mi walk

DOWNHILL SKI AREAS

A AFTON ALPS (pg. 88)

C COMO PARK SKI CENTER (pg. 90)

E MOUNT FRONTENAC (pg. 92)

G TROLLHAUGEN, WISCONSIN (pg. 94)

H WELCH VILLAGE (pg. 95)

I WILD MOUNTAIN (pg. 96)